EL INDIO

Diego Rivera. 3...

EL INDIO

by *Gregorio Lopez y Fuentes*

TRANSLATED BY ANITA BRENNER

Illustrations by Diego Rivera

FREDERICK UNGAR PUBLISHING CO.
NEW YORK

Printed in the United States of America

ISBN 0-8044-6429-4
Library of Congress Catalog Card No. 61-17563

Prefatory Note

WHEN the novel "El Indio" by Gregorio Lopez y Fuentes was awarded the National Prize of Literature—the first such award to be made in Mexico—the choice was an extremely popular one. Writing in *The New York Times* Book Review, Verna Carleton Millan said: "Gregorio Lopez y Fuentes has two qualities that are indispensable in a fine novelist: a warm, keen sympathy for mankind, coupled with an intellectual honesty that does not permit him to mar the sincerity of his work with sensational touches. For that reason 'El Indio' may be considered, along with Azuela's 'The Underdogs' and Guzman's 'The Eagle and the Serpent,' as worthy of being included in that very short list of books that have won an enduring place in Mexican literature."

In fact, all of Mexico is epitomized in this book—at least all essential Mexico. True, much is off stage as it were, but it is none the less here. Though the actual story encompasses only a comparatively few years, the Mexican drama from pre-Conquest days to the present is more than suggested with amazing economy of style in Lopez y Fuentes' pages.

"El Indio" is what one might call a composite novel. Not a single character is named, nor is the village which is the scene of the action identified. This will appear somewhat strange to American and English readers, but the innovation is a surprisingly successful one. Anyone familiar with the main outlines of Mexican history in recent times will be able to interpret the story in specific terms of what has actually happened and is still happening south of the Rio Grande. But any such explanations would seem pointless and unnecessary. "El Indio" can be enjoyed for what it is without straining for symbolism or historical analogies.

The translation presented certain obvious difficulties which only someone familiar with Mexico could solve. Though written in Spanish, the book contains many words which are not Spanish but Aztec or *Nahuatl*. This made a certain number of footnotes unavoidable.

8

PREFATORY NOTE

Lopez y Fuentes, who is still in his thirties, was born and grew up in a village in the State of Vera Cruz; and no doubt "El Indio" reflects to a large extent the scenes and impressions of his childhood. He had won a solid reputation in Mexican literature before the appearance of "El Indio," and is at the present time managing editor of *El Grafico*, a Mexico City daily.

LYNN CARRICK

January 9, 1937

EL INDIO

I. Gold

TERROR swept through the village when the three strange men appeared. At the first hut a woman dropped her cotton and spinning whorl. Another nervously untied the loom from around her waist, and, leaving the half-woven cloth, fled inside, slamming the door.

Ahead, the dogs barked. And the stampede to the near-by brush began: half-naked boys and ragged-haired women. It was the time of day when all the able-bodied men were in the fields.

The strangers came in pulling their horses along by the reins. Behind them followed a pack mule carrying two large boxes. Thus they had made the last stretch of their journey, over a trail hardly passable afoot, in search of this rancheria* nailed high in the sierra. The first of the strangers stopped and smiled, watching the natives run. He wiped his

---

* Rancheria—a small rural settlement.

forehead, and called his companions' attention to the effect of their arrival.

The village: one long alley of drab thatch houses grimed with smoke. In the black earth yards, plum trees, cedars, orange trees. On the low stone walls, clothes spread out drying. Beyond, the corrugated green of the sierra.

The three men looked at one another and felt sorry for the fugitives. One of them said:

"If they had a good road they would not be so backward. At least they'd be used to associating with the whites."

They went on up the street. At one of the houses, where the man ahead saw that the door had been closed from the inside and that therefore it was not deserted, he knocked softly. Nobody answered. The stranger, who was the guide of the party, knew the native tongue, and now resorted to it, giving his words the greatest possible gentleness, to inspire confidence.

"What are you saying to them?" one of his employers demanded.

"I am asking them for a little water."

Spoken in Aztec, the word opened the door. An

old man appeared, holding a calabash full of water. At the far end of the room, which was the entire house, there was a woman who had her back turned to them. From behind her legs a child peeped out as around a parapet. Timid but curious, he showed half his face, risking only one eye, bright as a cat's.

The strangers all drank from the same bowl. When the guide returned it and gave thanks, saying *tlazo-camati*, the Indian's face softened a little. He asked the interpreter who his masters were, what they were after, where they were going, and if they were not, perhaps, of those who many a time had done the natives so much harm. The white man explained: his masters had a few things to sell that might please the villagers; they were studying the countryside and, incidentally, sought a few curative herbs.

The guide turned to his masters and translated what had been said. Meanwhile, a few of the natives, seeing the old man talking to the strangers, had very cautiously opened their doors. Others had begun a wary return from the bushes to which they had fled. Heads here and there edged over the fences: black helmets of hair, brilliant eyes, pro-

15

truding cheekbones. The bold little boys came closer to admire the horses. The visitors sat on a wooden bench in front of the old Indian's house. Fatigued and perspiring, they fanned themselves with their hats. They were talking, apparently, of the place and its inhabitants and position, for their eyes ranged over the houses and hills, and now and then their gestures took in the old man at the door and the children in the street.

The interpreter turned to him again and asked if there were any place in the rancheria where the travelers might find lodging. The answer did not please the visitors, for the Indian said that as travelers never came here, there was no lodging; but, if they desired to remain where they were . . .

They said something among themselves and the invitation was then accepted. The guide and the old Indian unloaded the mule, then loosened the cinch. While the masters walked up and down the roadway, discussing something in a low voice and evidently much interested in the near-by hills, the servant plunged into a long conversation with the Indian. A hundred curious eyes looked on. After that he reported to the other white men:

16

Diego Rivera. 36

"I have questioned the old one carefully; he tells me there are no mines around here; as to the cache of gold, he insists he never heard tell of it; and that he knows nothing at all of gilded idols."

"You are a fool! Do you suppose he's going to tell you the truth right off like that? I have a description and a map of the place where these natives used to hide the gold dust they received as tribute. Here they accumulated the contributions of a hundred towns: gold dust in quills! Gold! Gold! And where did it come from? Mines in this very sierra! I have the map!"

In spite of his master's enthusiasm, the interpreter replied: "The old man says the tribe hasn't been here very long. Their ancestors, who were very powerful, lived in the valley, where they ruled over other tribes. Fleeing from the whites who persecuted them, they left the good lands of the valley and took these, which are hard, but safer."

"And what of it?"

"I mean, señor, that if their ancestors, those who were powerful, had their town in the valley, it is there we should look for the treasure."

"We will look here and we will look there, too.

19

The main thing is that we have reached the place shown on the map. And if that fails, we'll make these sphinxes give up their secrets! There is no use, though, expecting them to talk with big smiles on their faces; it will come out with pain. . . . Or, we may not have to do that. . . . What would you say if today or tomorrow somebody bought a string of beads or a bunch of yarn and paid us with a quill full of gold dust?"

∴

The men of the village heard about the whites when they returned from work at the end of the afternoon. They were drawn by the same curiosity as the rest to the dooryard where the merchants were displaying their wares.

The old man explained to his friends how the strangers came and what they were after. As to what they had for sale, there it was before their eyes. He warned them that they had been asking insistently about the *teocuitatl*,* the gold, to which he had answered that he knew nothing; and about

---

* *Teocuitatl*—Aztec word applied to gold, means literally "god's dirt."

the medicinal herbs, a question which all the old men in the council would have to decide.

The women were the most excited over the trinkets. The first one to buy, through the interpreter, a string of glass beads, had given the peddler money that made the three visitors look at one another, disgruntled. It was a perfectly ordinary coin. But other buyers perhaps would pay with gold dust or yellow counters, so they went on selling. Most in demand were beads of all kinds, yarn, and the *tochomite* * with which the native women work their cotton cloth and adorn their hair.

The men brightened up more when an elongated bundle was opened. Inside were horn-hafted machetes,† of the long kind that drag even when worn by a fairly tall man. Many of the natives bought these, but they always paid in common currency.

Trade was not giving what the merchants had hoped for, so the wares were put back in the boxes. They discussed their failure; there were still other things that could be tried. They inquired again

---

* *Tochomite*—a special kind of green yarn.

† Machete—a broad, heavy cutlass, principal tool and weapon of the Mexican peasant.

21

about the mines and gold caches from the men who were just getting home, who were more accustomed to whites from contact with them in the towns and haciendas. But they learned nothing.

Suddenly the watercolor sunset was blotted out. The shadow of the range advanced, and like a great stain moved on to cover the valley. The hens went to roost in the plum trees. The hogs, of the poorest breed—long, sharp snouts—bedded down in the sheds and against the stone fences.

Having left their animals tethered in an orchard, the two traders stretched out near their bundles, asleep or musing, while the guide wandered off.

And night caved in over the village. The distant green of the mountains disappeared, leaving only silhouettes cut against the sky. The houses became shadowy cones, with no more clue for the eye than the firelight through the chinks of the mud and bamboo walls.

Thus begins the sad evening of an Indian village: gray bundles squat in the doorways; women return from the well with their water jars on their heads; and from house to house comes the soft clap-clap

22

of tortillas * being made. There is the tireless wail of the sleepy child whose mother does not pick him up. Far away, the cry of the grouse and the bark of the dog in the cornfield. In the eaves, the circling flutter of bats.

The guide stopped at a door and asked for water. A furious watchdog obeyed his master and let him go in. While the water was being poured, the stranger took a quick look around. Three coppery boys slept, almost in a heap, on a *tlapextle*; † from a corner, two older ones stared at him with big surprised eyes; another ate his supper near the fire. The man of the house held the next to the smallest in his arms, and the woman, to give herself freedom of movement at her metate, ‡ had the youngest slung on her back.

The intruder drank, then remarked with amazement on the number of offspring. And the native, smiling, explained suggestively:

---

* Tortilla—classic native Mexican bread made of maize, shaped by patting the dough with the hands. It is about the size of a pancake and is baked on a griddle.

† *Tlapextle*—rope and bamboo mat laid across wooden supports; the typical Mexican peasant bed.

‡ Metate—three-legged utensil for grinding maize, used by Mexican peasants from time immemorial; most frequently made of porous lava-rock.

"Yes, many children. The torch or the candle burns down early. It gets dark, so what else is there for the poor to do?"

As the guide turned to leave, the woman rose, and her figure made him think of the saying, "The brood, hale; and the hen, stale."

Down the street an old Indian sat in the door of his hut and played a still older harp, held between his knees; a muted, ingenuous tune like a simple dance. His sons were shelling ears of corn inside, and the women, with nothing else to do apparently, ground away at the metates.

The music was so soft that a few steps away one heard it no longer. On rainy nights the chorus of the frogs in the puddles would surely mix with the notes of the harp, so that one could not be told from the other.

Some of the houses were already dark. The guide smiled, remembering the explanation he had just heard of why Indians have so many children . . . equally true of all poor people. Then he went back and joined his employers.

They were having their supper by the light

24

of a torch and the moon. The natives stared amazed at the way they opened small metal boxes and took their food out of them. The old man of the house gave them hot tortillas, and a clay dish full of chili almost to the brim. In return, his guests made him a present of some slices of ham. The old man showed the gift to his wife and sons, but no one tasted it, all preferring instead a tortilla rolled around a pinch of salt, alternating with bites of chili. Teeth dug in, the perfect teeth of herbivorous people.

While the strangers were putting their bedding down in the corridor, the interpreter again reported:

"They certainly do know it, but it is hard to make them disgorge their secrets. They are taught the tradition when they are children, and are commanded to keep it to themselves. I know of one stranger who tried to find out the secret of how the natives cure baldness, for there are no bald Indians —an herb that grows in certain spots in the sierra— and the man who had the recipe let himself be killed rather than reveal it."

"We shall see!"

25

Away off somewhere, there was the piping of a *chirimia*,* shrill and monotonous, something like a cricket.

----

* *Chirimia*—ancient Aztec wind instrument, like a flute.

II. Mestizos

DAWN breaks in a Mexican village with the glow of fires through the cracks of the walls. The women begin to prepare breakfast and the midday meal for the men. Once the fire is started, they come out with their baskets of *nixtamal* * held high like a tray, and their water jars on their heads. They go down to the spring that bubbles through the roots of some leafy *jalamate*.† There they wet their faces and arms, wash the boiled maize, and fill the water jars. Meanwhile, in the gray light, the men sharpen their machetes on the rough stones driven deep in the ground near the houses.

The handclapping of the tortilla-makers is heard again. In each house a man sits by the fire and eats his breakfast.

---

* *Nixtamal*—maize boiled and ground to the consistency of dough, from which tortillas and other Mexican breads are made.

† *Jalamate*—also *amate* or *amatl,* a tree that grows in the water. From its white bark the ancient Mexicans made the paper for their hieroglyph-literature.

Some seem to ruminate slowly and silently; they are the ones who are going to work in their own fields. The others, who have to be in the haciendas at sunrise, and those who have jobs to do for the authorities in the town, breakfast rapidly.

Each woman, meanwhile, puts up the midday lunch: tortillas, a piece of chili, a pinch of salt; and her man again sharpens the machete on the stone set haphazardly into the ground. In the orchards, the half-wild roosters crow hoarsely, and a little later, still in the dim light, the workers silently start down their separate trails.

∴

The paths that the Indians took from the village soon became barely perceptible furrows. They were like arteries, thick at the source and feathering out at the ends.

The men moved lightly toward their daily tasks. Some went through the woods until they reached the clearing made in several days of labor with machete and ax. Here they hung the food-sack on a limb, and resumed the job of cutting down the forest. In a few days the brushwood would be com-

28

pletely dry. They would then burn it. New earth and ash would guarantee a good crop.

Later, when the plants were in leaf, and bowed in green waves by the wind, the natives, bending in the furrows, would pull out the weeds that robbed the maize of the earth's nourishment. How the reddened midsummer sun would blaze down on those backs! The only comforts would be the light breeze that would sometimes dry the sweating foreheads, and the water-gourd whispering on their lips.

And, as the days went by there would come the harvest, when the Indians industriously co-operated to bring in the crops with all speed before the rains could wipe out their labor. Then they were happy; and even the women would go out and come back from the fields, doubled under the weight of harvest and child.

The others, day-laborers on the haciendas, had much farther to go. Day after day at sunrise they were already at the fringe of the master's corn or cane field. To sow, they would place themselves like athletes who are going to take part in some event that requires precision and discipline rather than strength and daring. A well-aimed thrust

29

with the planting stick, maintaining the symmetry of the rows; the second man takes his distance from the first, and the third from the second. They all make the same uniform movement of the arm, and with the same gesture drop the grain without losing a kernel; then take the same long step, measure and proportion for the next plant.

At the end of the day there would be a few cents and a mouthful of aguardiente.* In bad times the maize only and, if the master was generous, the drink besides.

In the grinding season, they would arrive armed with short machetes, preferably the kind that is hooked at the point and known as *huingaro*, because it does duty for the hand, and protects it from snake-bites in the thickest growths.

They bound themselves out by the week on the haciendas. From Sunday to Sunday their life would be nothing but cutting cane, feeding it to the mill, keeping the fire going, seeing that the boiling syrup did not overflow, feeding the work animals, and packing the brown sugar. Before dawn,

---

* Aguardiente—literally, "fire-water," usually applied to cheap raw brandy or straight alcohol.

they would be hitching the teams to the grinding mill and after dark they would just be coming back from the waterhole. At the end of the week their wages would not be enough even for un-bleached muslin to make pants and shirts for their sons, and they would receive that much only in case the job was not supposed to cancel some ancient debt. There was always the same disproportion between income and needs: forever ahead, the same receding lure. Thus, in good times; but, when drought kills the crops, the peon hears the same thing everywhere—there is no work.

∴

It was now broad daylight and the youngest of the knickknack peddlers stood in the arroyo near the spring washing his hairy arms. At that distance from the village this man with his high boots, rid-ing breeches and gun, was disquieting enough to make many women turn back with empty jars.

But one light-footed girl did not notice the stranger, and went as far as the well. She plunged her hands into the running water and washed them leisurely, seeming absorbed in her own reflection. She scooped water up to her face and smoothed her

31

sleek hair over her ears. As she bent over, her black braids swung down, and in the same move- ent her blouse and bead-embroidered *quexquemetl* * fell forward and showed the curve of her breasts.

She was standing in the water rubbing one foot against the other, when suddenly she became aware of the stranger a few steps away, staring at her. His eyes, particularly the expression in them, alarmed her.

He gestured, indicating a near-by hill. She pre- tended she had not seen and hurriedly picked up her water jar. The stranger put his hand on her arm. She wrenched herself from him sharply. The jar fell and was shattered on the rocks. The man murmured something that she did not understand, but there was meaning enough in his eyes and his loose lower lip to fill her with panic.

She tried to get to the step hollowed out of the bank, but he blocked her way. Then she bounded across the arroyo, seeking safety on the other side, and the stranger went after her. Then they raced like two deer when the doe, not yet in heat, rejects the stag.

* *Quexquemetl*—traditional Aztec garment, something like a tri- angular shawl.

Barefoot though she was, the girl ran very swiftly over the rocks, and the man was slow in overtaking her. For an instant only, he managed to grasp one arm; but with a supreme effort she slipped away. In frantic hope her eyes turned toward the houses, seeking protection. Yet, terrified as she was, she did not scream, as if the silence of her race had imposed itself even in such crucial moments. She fled finally in the direction of the hill, apparently certain that the road to the village was already cut off by her pursuer. Running at full speed, the two disappeared in the thicket.

And now screams echoed through the hills. Almost simultaneously—perhaps because the alarm had been raised already—six men crossed the arroyo, drawing their machetes and brandishing clubs. Panting like dogs on the track of their quarry, they reached the woods, and the stranger emerged, with a revolver in his hand. One of the natives moved toward him threateningly and he fired into the air. The avengers drew back.

Thus, with gun cocked, he marched to the arroyo, jumped across, and then went to look for the other whites at the house where the three had spent the night. While on the other side of the woods, the girl turned homeward with her face covered up by her hands. The men of her tribe followed, mute and somber. She had been rescued, but not avenged.

∴

The offense rankled. When the traders again spread their wares, no one came near them. The interpreter went from house to house, offering the things that had been most in demand the day before, but the doors were shut in his face. All the old men gathered in one of the houses to discuss what the tribe should do.

The visitors then decided to push ahead with their search in the mountains; but the natives would scarcely answer their questions. The old man in whose house they were lodged would not talk to them either. His entire attention seemed to be fixed on the reed basket he was weaving. He sat on a chunk of wood, the basket between his knees, his hands twisting like big tarantulas spinning their webs.

The elder of the whites, evidently head of the expedition, meanwhile reprimanded the other for his

34

behavior which, he said, had made the natives angry
and hostile. He walked up and down nervously in
the little yard, looking toward the undulating green
of the range.

All of a sudden he slapped his thigh with the
gesture of a man who has solved his problem. He
pulled a bundle of papers from his pocket and put
one aside. Having read it, he turned to the interpreter and ordered him to find the authorities of
the place.

The old man of the house informed them that
there were no authorities here other than the *huehues*, the elders like himself. Unwillingly, he pointed
to a hut at the end of the street where they were sit-
ing in council. He himself had stayed home for
fear the whites might attempt some other outrage, this time on his own family.

The guide and the trader went toward the council house. When they knocked, a lean dog with
long, sharp ears came out and barked at them. The
door was opened by an old man whose head was
utterly white and whose face was as beardless as
a child's. His little jet eyes conveyed nothing. He
was like a bent and aged idol. Only his lips,

35

pulled down in the facial cast of grief, revealed sorrows. White teeth, even and closely set, showed when he spoke.

Some of the natives, who had already been on their way to work, now turned back, to wait in their houses for whatever was to come next. Everything was to be feared: the whites fingered their guns, but not a shade of apprehension appeared on the old man's face.

Soon a crowd made up mostly of boys had collected in front of the hut. The women looked on from the doors of their houses with anxious and curious eyes. The dogs glared at the strangers and barked insistently. There was a whole pack of them, for every Indian has at least one dog, but not one among them that anybody would want—they were all bony and skinny, appropriate symbols of the misery of their masters. Their snouts were sharp from constant, hungry snuffing, and their ears were peaked like a coyote's. Their bulging ribs rose and dropped in time with their barking.

A sense of dread, as of an unearthly night, hung over the rancheria.

The interpreter told the old man that his master

deeply regretted what had happened; that he realized their anger was justified; that the act was no more than a piece of youthful madness, that the offender would be punished severely, and that he asked their pardon.

The old man said nothing. Then the interpreter, prompted as before by the trader, notified him that if, ignoring their apology, the natives refused to assist in the search for medicinal plants, they would have to make use of a signed order that they had been given by the municipal president on instructions from very high up.

Fear, accumulated in centuries of subjection, forced the old man to talk at last. He asked what it was they desired. They said all they wanted was a guide, who was at home in the mountains, knew the plants, and was familiar with everything. The paper was held up superfluously in front of the old man's face.

The writing on it meant nothing to him, but the paper itself—even if it had been blank—was enough to frighten him: he had been told that it was an order, and he knew what had always happened when his people disobeyed orders.

37

Still, he made no decision, pointing out that he had no power to do so by himself, since the authority belonged to all the old men together. A few of them drew near; their eyes asked what new offense was going to be committed now, this time on the oldest of all. More were called, and the council went into session under a cedar whose shadow would have covered an assembly ten times this size.

Some of the younger council members protested angrily, and wanted to refuse the demands of the whites. It would be better, they said, to get all the men together and put the strangers to death. Another of the more excitable reminded them furiously that every time an outsider set foot in the place he brought harm with him, even though he was always treated with hospitality and respect. The speaker's rage was apparent only in the meaning of his words, and a slight trembling of his hands. His face remained as impassive as a lava mask.

But the paper won. The oldest *huehue* quietly retold the tale of their past sufferings, their wanderings in the mountains, their years of hunger, and all because the tribe had disobeyed the whites and

38

provoked their anger. So it was decided to give the strangers a guide.

They chose for this purpose a young man who, in height, build, and bearing, was a worthy survivor of a race once great and powerful.

III. Eagle Falling

THE three traders had turned explorers and were preparing an all-day trip. Their horses were tied under some trees. The interpreter was filling the provision sack. The older man was slipping a roll of papers into a metal tube, and at the same time, making sure his magnifying glass was in his pocket. The younger had taken a camera out of his bag and was about to try it out on one of the old men of the council.

Aware of the white's intention, the Indian quickly moved out of range; for they believe that a likeness in possession of an enemy gives him power over the original, and that any harm done to an image is felt by the living man. For the same reason, they never give their true names, believing that evil can reach them more quickly if someone who wishes to harm them knows what they are called.

The young man who was to guide the strangers

arrived just then. He was bareheaded—of what use is a hat in a jungle?—and barefoot. His long, loose cotton-cloth pants were rolled halfway up his thighs, and his shirt was open across his chest. With his wide steady gaze, his black straight hair like brush strokes above his eyes, his high-boned cheeks, and his smooth lips clamped, he was beautiful.

They started out. At the arroyo where the girl had been attacked that morning, the head of the expedition stopped his companions. He took out the map that held all his hopes, spread it on one knee, and studied it a while. Then he looked toward the hills and checked them with points on the map. Finally, with a gesture as of slashing the mountain, he indicated the direction they must take.

The native started down a trail. The explorers followed. They all disappeared into the forest, under the eyes of the old men, women and children who had gathered to see them off. Very soon afterward, the man with the map objected to continuing on the path; he seemed to think that the Indian was attempting to take them off their course. He instructed the interpreter accordingly, at the same time repeating his previous gesture: a blow that sliced into the forest. The guide listened and then, unsheathing his machete, began to cut through the jungle.

How superbly he handled that blade! He swung it, effortlessly it seemed, cutting down boughs dangerously covered with thorns, slicing creepers out of the path, and pounding dead tree trunks, on constant guard against snakes possibly hidden inside and ready to strike at the heel.

They had barely penetrated the thickest growth when the whites stopped to examine a plant that attracted them. Meanwhile the guide took off his shirt and tied it around his waist. As they started again, the men behind him could not help but admire his body, supple rather than brawny. Not the bulging muscles of the athlete; but what endurance on the trail and at his work! When he gripped his machete to strike, his forearm became a knot of tendons. Copper engraved by labor and sun. Sculpture in motion, made of new cedar.

The interpreter was the most nervous of the three whites. He seemed to fear snakes especially, talked to his masters a great deal about snakebite, and asked the guide to show him which plant cured it. The young man said there was no need to ask; if he would just watch what the eagles did when they were bitten, he would know the remedy. At least, so the old men said: that animals know by instinct where to find food, where they are safest, and where the traps of their enemies are; whereas man knows nothing. But the interpreter insisted, so the guide showed him the first plant that happened to catch his eye.

At a place where the foliage opened out like a skylight, the head of the expedition stopped to look at his papers again. They were right on their course, he said, and had now gone about halfway.

No special circumstance, but rather the general friendliness of the guide, now encouraged the explorers to give vent to their greed. They had talked last night of the wonderful plant the natives knew for curing baldness; so the interpreter was told to inquire about it.

The guide looked at the strangers' heads and answered that, since they all seemed to have plenty of hair, he wondered at their concern. They insisted, however, telling him among other things that

43

the remedy was for a bald relative; so the boy pointed to a near-by plant with his machete. The whites then gathered a large bundle of these plants.

The great variety of birds seemed to interest only the Indian who, now and then, so they would not be frightened, whistled like them. Nor did the insects attract much attention, except for the mosquitoes. These had reddened the necks, ears and hands of the strangers, while the Indian seemed oblivious to them. Finally they came to the place where the map indicated that the mine or the caches of gold-dust tribute would be found. The eldest of the whites kept picking up stones and examining them under his magnifying glass. Some he split open and looked at more carefully, but did not find inside the longed-for glitter that would betray the presence of metal.

Tired and sweating, the three whites sat on a volcanic boulder and held a long discussion over the map. As often happens, the lines so precise on paper had become so vague in the field that they wished they had the draftsman there. The only conclusion they came to was that the mine had to be found.

44

The sun now poured down through the trees in vertical shafts. The walk had made them hungry, so they stopped to eat before resuming the search. When they finished, they offered the Indian what was left over, a can containing a piece of meat in oil. He smiled his thanks, but refused, and went on digging a tunnel in an ant hill with a stick.

With the meal and the heat they were in no hurry to go on. The interpreter suggested that they try then and there to make the Indian tell them the secret of the hidden gold. But the head of the expedition objected. It would be better, he said, to use up all the peaceful methods first, since he still hoped to find the clue in his papers.

When they started again, the guide noticed that his companions had lost so much enthusiasm that they kept making him stop and wait for them, even though he consumed a great deal of time as it was, in cutting through the woods.

They were heading toward a high hill. On one side of it there was an enormous apron of rock, looking something like a quarry. Here, perhaps, fierce waters pounded when the world was young.

A dark spot, like the entrance to a cave, showed through the sparse vegetation where the cliff-like formation began.

This site corresponded with the zone on the map. The head of the expedition felt sure it must be the place they were looking for: beyond a doubt, the gold or the mine was in that cave. He knew so little about such matters that the mere opening brought to his mind everything he had heard about the discovery of rich lodes.

But it was a difficult climb. They had to get through the forest that flung itself forward to the first spurs of rock; then through the dense thorny undergrowth and up the open slope littered with volcanic boulders that had split off the top during the rains. The guide made his way very easily, but the rest had to pull one another up by the hands. During the hardest stretch, they made the Indian help them with a long rope that the interpreter had brought along wound around his waist.

At the foot of the quarry they reached, exhausted, a deep ravine that could not be seen from the woods. The only vegetation in this miniature valley was a tubular ceiba tree with a branch, curiously like an arm, thrust out from its trunk near the ground.

They sat down to rest by the trunk, which was studded with thorns shaped like thumb-tacks. From here they had a good view of the country: the sierra unfolding in great plains on every side, the precipices like springboards for giants, and back of the hills, more hills, a succession of heights upon heights. And lost among them, the hope of finding the treasure guarded so jealously for generations.

The opening they had seen from the woods was the one thing left to explore. It was only about a hundred yards away, but the canyon and the rocks, piled up unsteadily and always threatening to slide, made a perfect defense. Beyond, the rivers in the valleys were like silvery snakes quietly warming themselves in the sun. The young Indian leaned against a sharp-edged rock and also looked far away. He was breathing easily, as if he had come up the hill without effort.

A half-hour later they decided to go the rest of the way. The Indian reached the mouth of the cave first, helped the others up with the rope, and

47

the three whites then went inside. They were a few meters deep when one of them lighted a match so they could find their way in the darkness. A swift flutter of wings struck them. It was made by big bats, fleeing from the invaders of their retreat.

The men came to the end of the cave very quickly. When they were back in the light again, they examined some objects that they had picked up inside. They thought they had found some gold dust; it proved to be bat droppings. And the stones they had brought out to look at closely were as ordinary as the cliffs they had scaled with so much difficulty. The three men gazed at one another, disappointment on their sweating faces. The crows swung above them, shrieking to their young. With some difficulty they made their way back to the place where they had rested a short while ago—the gully where the solitary ceiba tree grew. The oldest of the traders turned to his party and pointed to the vast panorama: all peaks, for the wall of the canyon shut off their view of the valley, and at the same time hid them from the rancheria. The white man's gesture could not have been more despairing. It was like a surrender of the will that had

48

organized the expedition. He had said with assurance that he would penetrate to the most secret fold of the range searching for the treasure that he had always looked upon as his own. It all looked easy enough at a distance; but what a difference when the legs weaken with fatigue, and the sun stings the back, and the rough ground seems unending.

Angry, he ordered the interpreter to question the Indian about the thing that was the real object of this journey. He said to tell him that they were not looking for medicinal herbs at all, but for mines and the gold-dust cache, the hidden treasure of his ancestors. The shadow of a smile appeared on the guide's face in answer; but he said nothing. The interpreter insisted, reminding him that these tribal secrets are put on the lips of children and that he, a grown man, must surely know them. The Indian again showed his white teeth; but still he said nothing.

The interpreter, prompted by the eldest white man, promised the guide a good share of the treasure if they could find it. But the young native repeated, in the same tone and with the same smile, that he knew nothing. The head of the expedi-

49

tion was furious; he sprang to his feet and, before the Indian could move, he pushed a revolver against his chest. The youth did not budge; maybe because he did not realize the danger, though the hammer was being pressed slowly upward in the nervous grip of the trembling hand.

"Tell him to talk, or I'll kill him!"

"You'd better talk," the interpreter said, "or this *coyotl* * is likely to kill you."

Indifferent apparently, the Indian remained silent. The white man gave orders to tie his hands behind his back. This was done with a belt. Then the rope was thrown over the ceiba branch and looped in a slip-knot around the guide's neck.

The white man, sure that the guide was helpless, put his gun back in the holster, and told the interpreter to resume the questioning. He thought that the preparations for torture might have more effect than the pistol threat. But it was no use, and only precipitated the whole sequence of events: the three men pulled at the end of the rope and lifted the youth a meter off the ground. When they

---

* *Coyotl*—literally, Aztec word for coyote; idiomatically used to mean white man. *Coyome* is a variation on the same root, and with the same meaning.

lowered him, he staggered like a drunkard, and would have fallen if the rope had not held him up.

"Talk!" commanded the interpreter.

Still the Indian did not answer. So he was raised again and this time kept in the air longer. At the first signs of strangulation, he was lowered, but now he was unable to stand at all, so they had to drop the rope. There were no signs of suffering on his livid face; only his hands quivered, still tied behind him. The interpreter knelt, took the rope from around his neck, and renewed the questioning: imperatively at first, then with persuasion and pity.

The young man's eyes were as serene as before the torture, when he had smiled at the interpreter's question. Now they turned slowly, studying everything around him. The treasure hunters, exasperated by the native's silence, and perhaps in order to decide on what to do next, moved away a little, talking in low voices.

They had gone some distance from him when the Indian, bound as he was, jumped up and ran toward the wall of the gully. He cleared it in two leaps, and emerged on the slope.

The three men dashed to the rock shelf and there,

as from a balcony, they saw the Indian plunging downward. At times he slid like a tree trunk propelled endwise from the peak. But, lacking the balance of his arms, he stumbled into a somersault rolling and bouncing down the slope, over the boulders that were like uneven battlements, until he vanished in the underbrush.

The whites must have lost their way back through the mountains, for it was dawn when they reached the rancheria. They said the boy would be there any minute. They saddled their horses and loaded their pack mule in haste, and left, not losing a moment.

IV. War

THE strangers appeared and disappeared at the turns in the road as they went down the slope. They were leading their horses along by the reins, as on the day before, when they had arrived. In the meantime a young man known as the *cuatitlacatl*, the hunter, had just reached the village.

He told the old men that he had been preparing a badger trap at the foot of a mountain when he heard something rolling down. It was something strange and did not sound like the stones that break loose during the rainy season.

When he went to see what was making the commotion, he found the white men's guide, lying still, all covered with wounds and bruises, with his hands tied behind his back. A thick bush had stopped him; otherwise who knows how far he would have gone crashing on.

The Indians, in the light of the business with

55

the girl on the day before and the sudden return and departure of the strangers, guessed what had happened. The hunter confirmed their suspicions. He told them that he had questioned the young man: he could hardly open his eyes, and just managed to say one word:

"*Coyome!*"

That was enough. He had been hurt by the whites. One old man, when he learned of it, began to scream and shout, blaming everything on the *huehues* for sending his boy with the strangers. His cries were like a call to war; the men ran to their houses for arms. Some came out unsheathing their machetes, others brandishing farm implements, and still others flourished fish spears as if they were lances.

The army consisted mainly of old men and boys, led by a few of the able-bodied men who had not yet left for work at this hour. The women trailed along with their littlest children, all gathering stones for the battle.

They crossed over ridges and cut through the brush to gain time and distance, making their way diagonally on the slope toward the steepest part of the trail. The crowd soon reached the level the whites were on. They were halfway down, and their horses were moving along the rocky ground with great difficulty.

Wild howls and a rain of stones from several directions opened the battle. The strangers sought shelter under a ledge of rock, while the natives manned several high vantage points and surrounded them. Stones shot from slings zoomed through the air. A spear, skillfully hurled, grazed the interpreter's forehead and buried itself in the flank of a horse.

The fugitives seemed to be hesitating about fighting back, for fear of a still more aggressive assault. They shielded themselves behind the horses and what natural barriers they could find. The projectiles showered by the natives soon made a miniature rockpile near them. The youngest of the whites was bleeding; a stone had struck his head. Hours passed before the natives, machete in hand, got ready to charge. Then the whites shot for the first time and forced their assailants to retreat a little. The volleys that followed were fired apparently just to frighten the Indians. But some were deliberately provoked by the natives with the idea of exhausting the whites' ammunition.

During a pause in the attack, the Indians saw the three besieged men confer. Evidently they had decided to break the siege by using their few remaining bullets. A new outcry went up when the Indians saw them mount and take the downward trail, digging their heels into their animals' flanks.

Another hail of stones, thicker and better aimed, fell on the fugitives, now no longer protected. But firearms beat back sling and spear. The yelling grew louder when the natives saw their enemies escaping. Then the ingenuity of war came into play: they began dislodging boulders, sending them rolling, in the hope that one of them would sweep the whites before it.

The huge projectiles bounded swiftly down the slopes, taking shrubs and smaller rocks with them. At each broadside the whites covered their heads with their forearms, as if that could protect them. One after another the rocks passed above them and hurtled into the depths; and each time, yells of delight rose from among the natives, who thought they had gained their end.

Diego Rivera. 36.

One of the smaller rocks turned out to be the best aimed. The natives seemed to have no doubt about it, for their excitement became intense the moment it started rolling. In complete silence all their attention was now concentrated on its trajectory. The rock passed just over one of the horses, without even touching the animal, and neatly swept the chief of the expedition with it: the projectile bounced the man in front of it like a fly hit by a boy's rubber band.

When the last echoes of the falling rock died away at the bottom of the canyon, the Indians started yelling again. And thus, satisfied with their revenge, they went back to their homes.

∵

All that night the rancheria buzzed with excitement. It was evident that the old men were in council, and the villagers crowded around them, droning like a disturbed beehive.

The men who had just returned from work were told what had happened. Those who had been in their own fields, those who had come up from the valley after their daily labor in the haciendas, and those who had just finished their week as servants in the houses of the rich townspeople—all heard, and gave their opinions, but they carried no weight. The council of elders would decide.

The most important information was brought by one of the Indians just back from service in the town. He had met two whites on horseback, one of them leading a pack mule, and the other a riderless mount. It was clear from this that the fugitive treasure hunters had abandoned the one who was hit by the rock—maybe buried under it—at the bottom of the canyon.

The old men remained sunk in thought for a long time. Beyond question the white man was dead; therefore, they could expect reprisals. The paper the strangers had shown them was proof that they had influential connections. And, just as they had been able to obtain credentials, so they would get an order to capture and punish the killers.

The oldest of the *huehues* got up from the stone where he had been sitting. The moon rose like a yellow mirror catching the fading light of the sun. The old man's eyes ran over the crowd.

Few, if any, were missing. He beckoned those

farthest away to come closer. They all looked alike in the first light of the moon. Their color was the same and their features identical, as if cast by one impulse, the reason for their meeting.

Everybody was silent as the old man spoke. He said the town would take its revenge even if the rancheria was in the right. As had happened before, the death of the white man would be a pretext for annihilation and pillage.

A new cycle of suffering had begun, he explained, and they could survive it only if the whole tribe faced it together, just as they had punished the white man together. He and the other elders, although they were part of the rancheria and had witnessed the act, could not say who pushed the rock that, plunging down the mountainside, had caused the death. Furthermore—and he raised his voice in resentment and anger—to give up the avenger would be an insult to the women of the tribe, for the pursuit of the girl was an outrage to all of them. Likewise, it would be an affront to the men, for the misfortune of the youth who served as guide through the mountains was an injury to them all.

The speaker concluded with an outline of his plan

63

of campaign: abandon the rancheria; take refuge in the mountains as in past epochs of persecution; resist when the situation was favorable; beware of the neighboring tribes whose hatred made them allies of the strangers; and finally, for whoever fell into the hands of the whites, this order—sealed lips. That was their strength!

"No matter," he told them, "if they burn your feet to make you confess our hiding-places. Not a word! If they hang you on a tree to tear from your lips the names of those who took part in the fight with the three whites—not a word! If they twist your arms till they break, to make you tell where we have our provisions—not a word!"

The *huehue* then turned to the other old men, and they nodded their heads in approval; for in his mouth, the tongue of experience had spoken. The crowd was silent. And silently they scattered.

That night the rancheria was emptied. The women went along the trails in the light of the full moon, carrying kitchen utensils in their arms and children on their backs. Behind them, the men led their sons by the hand, and brought along the fish nets, the machetes, and the blankets. By dawn only

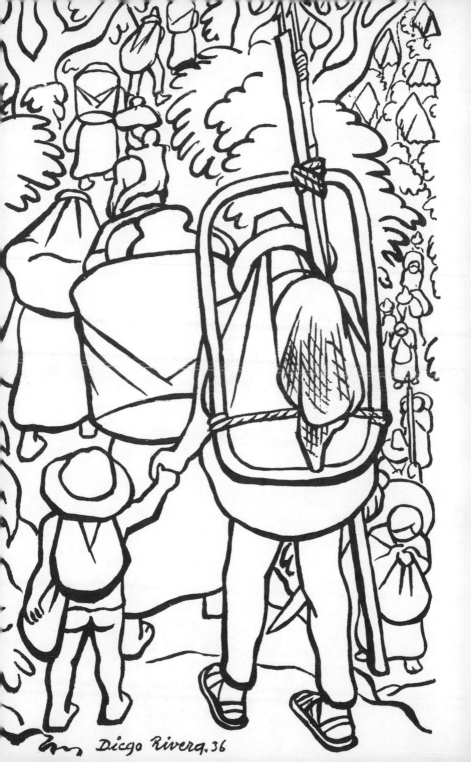

Diego Rivera. 36

a few of the braves remained. They had come back for part of the last crop and were leaving again. At sunrise, the old men filed out of the rancheria, after a night spent in council, lamenting the endless sorrows of their people.

V. Punishment

I N town the officials notified their superiors of the encounter, and were told to punish the offenders at once; so they quickly organized a punitive expedition to the village. This company consisted of police, some of the more aggressive townsmen, who joined with alacrity, the local schoolmaster, and the secretary of the municipal president. And the municipal president himself, riding his best horse, headed the little troop.

They divided themselves into three groups, with instructions to meet on the outskirts of the rancheria at about the time they would tread on their own shadows. The idea was to block all the roads by which the natives might escape—about like trying to bolt and bar the mountains.

Those who took the roughest trails dismounted and went on afoot. They all had their weapons ready, for the municipal president's orders were strict: fire on anybody who tries to escape; and if they put up a fight, wipe them out. Most of the company complained at the bad state of the roads and put the blame on the Indians for not having improved them in so many years. It was the first time the municipal president had set foot in the region and realized the misery of the natives he had been sent to pursue.

When the townsmen heard a horn blow the signals they had agreed on, they entered the rancheria. The streets were deserted and not a soul could be glimpsed through the doorways. All the houses were closed. There was not the slightest sign of a human being anywhere.

Here and there a cat, the animal that attaches itself to the house rather than to the inmates, hurled itself over a wall and raced into the woods. Even the trees in the orchards and yards were so still as to heighten the emptiness of the forsaken homes. The look that epidemics stamp on Indian villages, when the inhabitants are exterminated because of negligence, ignorance and helplessness, hung now over the cluster of hovels that the authorities had invaded.

The most aggressive did not wait to be told what

to do. They went right ahead, smashing the doors open in search of the "rebels." Finding no one, they picked up whatever appealed to their greed: a machete, a fishing net, a sack of beans or of maize, one thing or another of what little an Indian's house can contain.

Then they gathered in the little square where the fiestas and *tianguis* * take place during peaceful times. On guard against a possible surprise, they all kept their weapons in their hands, ready to fire. But, after a while, as no foe appeared, the townsmen decided to take a rest. The municipal president, his secretary, the schoolmaster, and two or three others seated themselves in the agreeable shade of a tree. There was no one in the drab huts around them, but the official and his cronies felt certain that several pairs of sharp eyes were watching them at close range from the heights.

Convinced of this, some of the whites began to shoot into the thickest woods on the near-by hills. Ten or fifteen weapons were fired simultaneously, producing a deafening noise and an echo that rolled from hill to hill for a long time. Few of the bul-

* *Tianguis*—market fair.

lets could be expected to find a target in that expanse; still, some Indian crouching in his hiding-place might have been hit. At least it was on that chance that the guns were fired.

The noise, in any case, frightened a cat that streaked across an alley. The municipal president's secretary aimed at it—there being no natives on whom to avenge the discomforts of the journey—and fired. The beast jumped grotesquely and kept on running. The secretary, with a reputation as marksman to maintain, said that obviously the cat had been hit—you could see that in the way it jumped; but, as cats have nine lives . . .

Dense smoke was beginning to issue from one of the huts; with it came some of the members of the expedition. In a very short time the walls, which were no more than sticks daubed with gray mud, were consumed in the fire. Rats and a few winged insects came out of the ruin.

Then it caved in. Only the distance between the houses kept the fire from spreading. Around it the spectators laughed and shouted.

The secretary, still annoyed at being pulled away from town where right now he would have been

71

playing billiards, began saying that Indians were unruly people, loafers, drunkards, and thieves. The president, a man of the same ideas, summed it up by adding that they were a disgrace to the country.

"What are they good for, since they oppose all progress? The practical and progressive men of other countries have done well to exterminate them. Race of inferiors! If the federal government would only give me the authority, I would march into all the ranchos with blood and fire, and kill them off like beasts of the jungle."

He said it resentfully, for part of his plan had been to carry off at least fifty native prisoners. And now they had slipped away from him. He repeated:

"*Si, señorés!* Like beasts of the jungle."

While he talked, he went through the motions of pulling an imaginary trigger. The schoolmaster, who was leaning against a tree and listening quietly and patiently to these harangues, spoke up then:

"Well, I have a different opinion. There are many theories about this question of the natives. I am going to tell you about them, leaving my own to the end. Some people think it is necessary to

Diego Rivera. 36.

colonize the biggest Indian settlements with whites in order to cross-breed them. They base their argument on the fact that we, the mestizos, are the products of cross-breeding and we are the most important and progressive element. Do with them as with the unpedigreed animals: cross them with superior specimens."

"A fine part you want me to play, señor professor," the president protested, but the schoolmaster went right on:

"Others consider that the problem can be solved with schools. Build schools everywhere. And it has even been said that much has already been accomplished; but that is because in the city they confuse in the one word peasant, both the mestizo and the Indian, without stopping to think that the first, because of his language and tastes, is already one of us; whereas the Indian is separated from us by a high barrier, that of his language and traditions. Those who uphold this idea have created the word 'assimilation'; but to accomplish that, we need more than schools."

The president replied:

"Those are all sentimental ideas. Just try educat-

75

ing the Indian and then we'll see who's left to till the soil! If we don't exterminate him, then the one thing to do is to leave him just as he is, working for those of us who are his physical and intellectual superiors. The proof that they won't yield to any peaceful means is right here—the people of this rancheria have run off rather than obey the rules of law and order."

"Here is my theory, *señor presidente*," the teacher continued. "The fact that they have fled to the wildest part of the sierras shows only one thing— that they do not trust us; that even if they had been told the authorities were coming just to investigate, they would not have waited. The truth is this: they have a profound distrust of us, stored up through the centuries. We have always deceived them and now they believe in nothing except their own misfortune. They see an executioner in each of us. They mistrust us on a scale that begins at the lowest levels of the valley, and reaches from the edges of the rivers to the highest peaks of the mountains. When they were free they lived where we now live. To the degree that they were ex- ploited and deceived, they climbed as if escaping

76

from a flood, until they came to where they live now. They think they are safe here because we are too lazy to go after them."

"And your theory?"

"My theory rests on precisely that, on restoring confidence. How? By kindness, because fortunately the Indian is appreciative. We should treat them in a different way, attract them by giving them some real help and not the sort of protection that has always been aimed at keeping them alive in order to sweat them as if they were work animals. And for all this, there is nothing like roads. But not those that go through the valley to connect the cities; link the rancherias instead. Highways teach the language better than schools. Then bring the teacher. But he should be some one who knows the customs and feelings of the Indians, and should not try teaching them exactly as if they were whites. Given all this, they would work much better—either on the land they have or the land that would be given to them."

Suddenly yells from the doorway of a house where some of the expedition had taken possession cut the schoolmaster's speech. Everybody turned to

77

look toward a clearing that was like a postage stamp, high on the slope of the nearest mountain. An Indian was running across it—a hunter maybe. Some of the townsmen aimed at him.

The president jumped to his feet, threw his hand up as if to ward off a blow, and shouted:

"Don't shoot! Don't shoot!"

They all stood and watched the dark figure reach the end of the clearing and enter the woods. Then the president sat down again and began to talk:

"Professor, you never said any of this before. I am very much impressed by your theory; so much that I am beginning to regret this chase. I am distressed by the orders I have been carrying out so enthusiastically. They tell me there is quite a stir in the city about this white man who came to look for medicinal plants for the good of humanity and was sacrificed by savages. They are even proposing to make a statue of him and name a street in his honor. Just the same I have a feeling in the bottom of my heart, that they must have done something to these natives to make them attack; for there is no denying the patience of the native race. . . . Our race!"

78

Hearing the president talk in this vein, the secretary, who was stretched out on the ground, jumped up excited, planted himself in front of the others, and said:

"I am indeed astonished, *señor presidente*, by the change that has come over you, just because the professor said a few words. You, too, begin to talk of the race . . . our race! . . . Your race maybe, but not mine! What makes it a 'race'? They are tribes! *Si, señor*, isolated tribes, numerous though they may be."

The schoolmaster went on with his argument calmly:

"Simply because they are isolated by the enormous distances, and the lack of highways, and because it is impossible for them to maintain bonds that have been broken by ignorance and slavery, this does not mean that the race has been destroyed. It has its traditions, somewhat sidetracked perhaps; its physical traits, customs and spirit; and though much weakened by subjection and exploitation, it exists, and only needs to be reclaimed."

"Words, man! How can it be a race if some of them talk one language here, eight journeys to the

79

west they talk another, and fifty kilometers to the north they have still another language—or rather dialect—that none of the others understands? They are tribes!"

"Descended from a single trunk: a race, even though they speak different languages."

"Go on! A race in fragments, almost completely scattered, without bonds among itself, ignoring itself completely, without knowing in what part of the country there are other men who would even understand its words!"

"I'll give you an example to disprove that: Is it necessary for the existence of a race of setters that they know where there are others like them, and exchange correspondence with them?"

"That's very different! What is there in common between the Otomi, who live on the central mesa, who struggle against the cold, drinking pulque, and sleeping in ashes, who live in sheds roofed with maguey waste and eat reptiles and bugs, and the Totonac, of clean customs and brilliant past? What affinity do you find between the taciturn Tepehua and the pig-headed and quarrelsome Huichole? The inhabitants of this very region, descended from a strong branch, the Nahoa, do they even know the name of the rancheria inhabited by others like themselves on the other side of the sierra?"

"That just proves that we have had them bowed over the furrow so long that they haven't had time to look at the horizon."

"Right here, among the neighboring rancherias, are there any links strong enough to make a union worthy of a race?"

"Because we have taken it upon ourselves to sow discord. It has been a policy, many times not even conscious, which has blocked an inter-tribal understanding that showed itself first in race war. That's why we are here today, and if you want to convince yourself, señor secretary, ask after the fugitives in any rancheria, and see if anybody tells you. Among themselves they may be divided, but against us they will always be together."

"Well, the history of the Conquest tells us otherwise. The best allies of the Conquistadores were the natives themselves against their brothers!"

"That was different. As the circumstances were different. And don't spout history at me! I have

81

studied it and I have lived it. When the Indians attacked the town years ago, I was one of the defenders. When they were preparing the assault, we noticed a few suspicious details, but not a soul betrayed the secret. We began to observe only that the Indians no longer came to the *tianguis*, that they stopped their daily labor in the haciendas and that the Indians drafted by the authorities for weekly service did not come when they were called. Some, who were captured, in spite of threats and the strongest means of making them talk, confessed nothing, even though they belonged to rancherias divided by the bitterest feuds."

"And what does that prove?"

"That the idea of shaking off our yoke had begun to spread among them and had wiped out their feuds; in a word, that the *nantli*, the nation, their race, was taking shape. When they attacked the town they were possessed by an insatiable spirit of vengeance. In their fury, they did not even spare the children, nor the old men, nor the women. All were put to the knife. They wanted to exterminate us. Then, with fire, they tried to wipe out even the last traces of our homes. The slaughter was

82

frightful. Thanks to the superiority of our weapons and the opportune aid of the soldiers, they were beaten back. Some prisoners were hanged at the edge of the town as an example to the rest: they all died bravely, uncomplaining, haughtily proud. The retribution was bloody. We razed whole rancherias. Finally, nearly all the leaders fell into our hands, and we hanged them or shot them. They said that the chief, a young Indian, died in a skirmish, but that is not true. Because he was the most important, or because in him still rested the hope of the race, he managed to escape by pretending to be one of the fallen in the struggle, and went to hide in the mountains, and stayed there. There are those who say that they have seen a copper-skinned man, who looks more like a savage, going swiftly along the roads. He is a hunter, and it is believed that his brothers protect him. We have heard that this strange creature comes at night furtively into the rancheria, talks to the old men, and before dawn returns, austere, to the mountains, as if somehow he were freedom itself."

"Old wives' tales, professor!"

The municipal president, who had dropped out

of the discussion, seemed to be rested a little, for he had stopped fanning himself with his hat.

All of a sudden he rose and, ordering his horse to be brought, he began to make ready to go back to the town. Those who had left their mounts scattered along the trail took the footpaths, while the president and his group went to the road over which they had come that morning. They rode off in the freshness of the late afternoon, when the ripe sun was falling beyond the sierra.

VI. Submission

WEEDS grew in the streets of the rancheria, and spread to the doors of the houses, as if the forest were reclaiming that which man had usurped many years before. On moonlight nights the place looked the same as always, but the silence was much more intense: not a cock crowed, not a dog barked.

On one of these clear nights, a man was heard persistently calling from somewhere below the mountain. It beat his voice back in the silence like a great sounding board. The huts and caves on the hills were the thousand ears of a fugitive tribe: they heard the message, but gave no answer. The calling went on all night. Some of the words rang out clearly: peace, pardon.

It was a messenger from the government authorities who came to propose the return of the Indians. Excitement, curiosity, and hope of peace must have spread through the sierra. The old men, the run-

85

ners, and the warriors may have gone back and forth through the woods, exchanging opinions as to the possibility of an agreement. But in the night no one appeared in the rancheria to confer with the messenger of the whites.

The sun was already high when one of the old men came down from the nearest mountain on the side of the arroyo, and cautiously approached the peace delegate. They talked under the same cedar where the council of elders had decided to flee to the forest with the whole tribe. The old man showed him his clothing, all in tatters: the women had not been able to get cotton for their looms. Then, pointing to the fields, he told the messenger to look at what had been cultivated ground and was now full of weeds; not a beanshoot, not a spear of maize.

The messenger was moved. He was an Indian from another rancheria, and read in the old man's words the lament of a tribe that had suffered hunger. He explained that his mission had been delayed by the many difficulties of getting in touch with the tribe. The people of the town, he said, had forgotten everything, and the authorities no longer de-

86

manded that the death of the white man be punished.

He made no attempt to cover up the real reasons
for the peace overtures. As he understood it, the
townsmen were asking for *semaneros*,* the hacienda
owners demanded workers for the sugar mills, the
traders complained that the customers in the *tianguis*
were few, and the inhabitants of the other rancherias
had protested because the entire burden of repair-
ing the roads, after the rains, fell upon them. In
short, the people of the village were needed; hence
peace was proposed.

In the light of the old man's experience, these reasons were much more convincing than all the promises of pardon. He thought they might come to
terms. He weighed matters rapidly and with confidence; if they were needed, there would be no difficulties, nothing to fear. In the years that had
made his hair white, he had learned only too well
that the *gente de razon* † made only two gestures

---

* *Semaneros*—Indians drafted by the week for domestic service in
the houses of the town officials and influential citizens.

† *Gente de razon*—literally, people of reason; idiomatically, what
the whites and mestizos generally call themselves to distinguish themselves from the Indians.

toward them: with one hand they gave, and with the other they took.

But he did not decide at the moment. He said he had authority only to listen to the proposals, and told the emissary to come back the next night. The two men said good-by to each other fraternally; and while one took the road to the valley, the other climbed the trail toward the peak.

∵

They met again punctually. Before the old man had spoken, the emissary gave him a present sent by the authorities for all the *huehues:* a bottle of aguardiente. The answer of the tribe was favorable. They accepted the proposals, but with the condition that the whites stay away from the rancheria, for the Indians did not trust them.

∵

They started back to their huts that same day; first, however, fumigating them with copal * to expel the evil spirits that might have taken possession during their long absence. Busily the men cleared

---

* Copal—aromatic resin used by the Indians of Mexico ceremonially and medicinally.

Diego Rivera. 36

the weeds from the yards and the streets; industriously the women swept their homes.

The next day an order arrived demanding workers to serve in the houses of the town's influential citizens, and others for the sugar mills on the haciendas.

And, as they kept coming back from their tasks, unharmed by the whites, confidence began to grow again where the weeds had flourished. The tribe had returned to its life of tranquil isolation.

∵

But their economic condition did not improve for several months; they therefore had to put up with much the same hardships as when they were refugees in the forest. The fields had lain fallow, so there were no crops.

The maize, which they got by bartering their labor in the near-by ranches and haciendas, was mixed with ground roots and the tenderest papaya bark. It was some time before their regular diet included beans. The pods, that filled out with the rains, were harvested before they were ripe.

Thanks to these early crops and the timely rains, many families that had been preparing for weeks to

91

migrate in spite of the *huehues'* decree to the contrary, now changed their minds. They had wanted to go and look for better land, farther away from the whites, and protected by some friendly tribe that had not suffered so much.

The old men had argued that their gods lived in these hills which they were planning to abandon. They cited their recent victory over the whites, who in the end had to ask for peace first. They listed all the favorable signs of the first rain; and, finally, they pointed to the fields already under cultivation, with all the prospects of a good crop.

But while they waited, the natives had to look for wild fruits, as in the days when they were persecuted. They grew much more interested in hunting; and every day many families turned to the river for their food supply. If they had felt more confident, they would all have gone down to the valley to ask for work among the mestizos. But they were still afraid.

Then the earth, more fertile than ever, as if to make good the arguments of the old men, yielded as much in a single crop as it had before in three; and with only one rain.

VII. The Tablet of the Law

IT was a Sunday lighted with gold.

A murmur of voices wound down the rough path that drops from the sierra and cuts through the highway to the plains.

Words strung out like beads came echoing with mysterious overtones in the lonely forest. They suggested a scene like the chromos of the Day of the Dead that one finds in the houses of country people: a procession of mourners, carrying lighted candles and palms; sorrow on some faces, resignation on others.

How that picture stamps itself on the imagination of the children on the day itself when the dead are given offerings of what is consumed by the living. It becomes a caravan winding through dreams. And, under the spell of folk tales, the murmur of the procession moving with palms and candles is heard at dusk among the fields.

93

That is what the voices descending from sierra to plain were like. They were the souls of a race. As they came closer, the words of a tongue with no *r*'s, a tongue fluid with the undulations of *l*'s, came clearer and clearer.

Through an arched opening in the foliage they could be seen as they came along the path. They were walking in single file, all barefoot; so that only the occasional crackle of a dry leaf betrayed their hurry. One young man, with his trousers rolled up, leaving his muscular legs bare, went by in quick strides. He had a long pick on his shoulder, and looked as if he were off to war. A lively small boy, very sure of himself, and armed with a stick, followed: he was as shock-headed as a bear and his nose was like the beak of an eagle. Next came an old man leaning on a staff: white head bare, not noticing the leaves above because his eyes were fixed on the ground. He moved along with the same dogtrot that had eaten away a century of distances. Then, a tawny girl, her coppery skin glowing, her arms bare, her braids wound around her head and knotted in front, and her *quexquemetl* pinned on top of her head as a symbol of maidenhood. Her firm flesh rippled at each step. And finally, the mother: on her back a child; in front, and unseen, a child.

They passed and disappeared. Only thus, stealthily, can this race be seen at its full height. They are like all untamed animals. When they believe themselves alone, they draw up to their full size, but then at the slightest suggestion of danger, how they shrink! What timidity! Even the peccary is beautiful when it is free; the stag a sculpture in solitude.   ∴

Among the reeds, where sand clearings glistened in the sun, twenty families were preparing to fish. Men, women, and children were getting their gear in order, under the trees whose roots the last floods had stripped. The fish spears, some of them barbed, were being sharpened on the stones at the edge of the bank. An old man squatted, mending his cast-net, and all the boys were fastening pieces of sharp, pointed wire to the ends of their cane poles. Women were giving suck to their children. Others, having just put them down in the shade of the chaparral, were tying their nets around their waists to collect the silver-scaled trout.

95

They were all nearly nude. This is what the ancient *matlazincas*, the people of the nets, must have been like when they wandered uncertainly many centuries ago; when, on the trail of a chant which was also a portent, they went along the banks of the rivers, natural food stores for nomad tribes.

Down the river the sound of the falls could be heard. Upstream, the surface of the water was fringed with spray by the swift current. The fishermen had come to the best place for their meager equipment. Here the river widened out and was not very deep.

They all knew well enough that at this time of day the best fish were frisking where the current was strongest. Up the river there would now surely be trout in shoals, catfish in schools, and mullet splashing at the surface. On the other hand, where they were going to fish, their catch would necessarily be poor, like their resources. They would have to be satisfied with the bony porgy and the minnow. Before beginning their work, they stared hungrily at the rapids.

A bold-eyed youth came forward with the confession that he had a cartridge of dynamite, and sug-

gested the desirability of taking a chance. He said
he had already done it on moonlight nights when no
warden dares go out after trespassers. But the elders objected firmly and turned toward a near-by
rock on which there was a sign.

The markings on it had already been explained
to them: it was a warning; and, molded as they were
to obedience, and fearing punishment, they did not
want to disregard it. The inscription said:

> "By order of the authorities, fishing with dy-
> namite is prohibited in this precinct. Notice is
> hereby given that infractions will be punished
> by fifteen days in jail or a fine of twenty-five
> pesos.—The Municipal President."

A long, meditative silence was broken by an old
tlachisqui, a seer, who at the edge of the river
stretched his arms out in front of him, fixed his eyes
on the sun, and mumbled a prayer:

"Father of that which lives and that which does
not live: Lord of the earth, of the water, of the
wind, and of the fire: if you give food to the crow
and to the snake and to the tiger, give me some fish
for my children, and for the children of my children!"

97

He waded in up to his knees, taking a bottle that his wife handed him. Then he began to talk to the river itself:

"You go your way, and we are ants who remain here: now that your countenance is serene, hear me . . ."

The word *hueyeatl*, the sea, the father of rivers, was heard in the prayer. The old man half covered the mouth of the bottle with one finger, and let a few drops of aguardiente fall into the water. Then he drank: it was like an alliance sealed by a toast. Then they all came forward confidently into the river.

These were merely preliminaries. They began actual preparations by finding the shallowest place, where the water came about halfway up the leg. Here the strongest brought stones and piled up a low wall. The old men reinforced this improvised dam with branches and mud. The women and boys brought reeds and thrust them into the stone barriers. Narrow openings were left at intervals, through which the water flowed more rapidly.

How hard they worked! One would think there was no hot sun beating down on their shoulders.

The men seemed unconscious of their strength, and the women indifferent to their bare breasts: some firm, some flaccid. The boys were naked, brown as man before his first shame brought a blush to his clay.

Their main job was now finished. The men who had nets stationed themselves at the openings. The old men and the boys went and stood at each end of the dam, barring the places through which the frightened fish might escape. The full-grown men and the strongest women waded out into the stream to where the water reached their armpits. There they strung themselves out against the current.

Then the drive began. It was a splashing line, men and women wading almost elbow to elbow. The ones who brandished spears poked around among the large rocks, stirring up the slow-moving porgies. Some plunged new-peeled wands into the water to startle the fish with the white wood.

Those who had cast-nets were the nimblest; holding the middle between their teeth, and with the edges resting on the forearm, they were ready to cast at the first sign of quarry. Hemmed in, the fish began to zigzag past, whirling like small shadows

99

under the water. Suddenly one young man flung out his gig. It shook and then began to cut through the water, standing almost straight up.

What a hullabaloo! They all knew that there must be a fairly large fish at the other end of the stick, well able to bear its weight. Somebody grabbed it and held it skillfully, adjusting the tension to the movement of the fish. A sudden pull might let the fish escape.

The fish, smacking the surface of the water, turned over and over. Then the man ran a finger into its gills, and bit it in the head to kill it. He pulled out the spear, tearing the white flesh.

The fishermen who were catching their prey as it tried to go through the openings of the dam began to pull their nets out more frequently, emptying them into their provision sacks. Whenever a fish managed to jump over the dam and escape, or slipped through the barrier of legs, the shouting grew deafening.

The nets were thrown in and pulled out, abundantly full, but still not enough in proportion to the number of fishermen. The water, though free and flowing, became muddied at the place where the final drive was made. Then, even when the women dipped into the water with their carrying nets, they brought up minnows like new tin and sharp-finned porgies.

Now came the time to distribute the catch. Each emptied his harvest in a hollow that had been dug in the sand. The seer, squatting, put the big fish to one side. They had all contributed and all would share. The old man gave out fish according to the needs and the labor of each. Heads of families received portions for themselves and for their women and children.

Suddenly the entire tribe stopped, staring at the rock ledge up the river. Some horsemen had appeared. When they dismounted, the women and children scrambled into the bushes.

The natives knew at once, from the preparations made by the newcomers, that the river was going to be dynamited. They were amazed, knowing that it was forbidden: set forth, as had been explained to them, by the notice on the rock. But the strangers, who must have understood the astonishment of the Indians as they watched at a distance, and in order not to set them a bad example, turned the sign over. The other side said:

"By order of the authorities, fishing with dynamite is permitted in this precinct for a half-hour.—The Municipal President."

This action made it plain to the Indians that the horsemen must be the authorities themselves, as no one else would have the power to turn the sign. Certain of it, the old men drew near. What an air of protection and superiority was assumed by the functionaries! What painful humility on the part of the natives! Most of the tribe looked on without moving: faces peering, wide-eyed and excited, from the undergrowth on the bank.

Whoever had come with the authorities must be, they supposed, an important personage, for they knew that fishing parties such as this were always organized in honor of very distinguished visitors: Some of the natives made ready to gather the fish killed by the explosion. The carefully prepared cartridges of dynamite were then lighted, cigarette to fuse, and thrown out at spaced intervals.

There were three blasts; three great bulges rose

102

from the river so high that the water, pulverized as it came down, was swept by the wind like fine mist. The fish, big and little, fell in a glistening shower. By this method, the municipal president explained, even the fry are killed; that is the reason for the restriction—but in the case of visitors so distinguished . . .

What a choice and abundant catch! The president and his guest, tempted by the sunshine and the delightful water, which was as clear as an eye untainted by malice, went in to bathe. What bloated abdomens, and in what disgraceful disproportion with the arms and legs! When they tried to swim they flapped about grotesquely, supporting themselves with their hands on the rocks at the bottom.

When the party was ready to leave, the sign was turned back again to the side that said: "By order of the authorities, it is prohibited . . ." The seer and his people stood looking at the rock in silence; taking note, perhaps, of the inequality.

Shouts down the river broke into the silence. A small black head, the head of a child, was bobbing along, dragged by the current. They knew it was just a few meters away from the waterfall—death.

They all ran; the quickest plunged in swimming, the rest went over the rocks. When the child rose on the last turn, and disappeared in the falls, the wail of the tribe was like an ululating protest. Had they not made their offering to the river before they began fishing? What debt was being paid now?

The first to reach the place looked anxiously at the waters boiling, and making pillars of foam as they dropped. Nothing; but beyond, where the whirlpool eddied in widening circles, a dark head, the head of a child, moved clumsily toward the bank, with hands flapping very close to its face, swimming like a tired puppy.

The mother, who had stripped off her clothes as she ran, tenderly picked up the child, likewise nude; and the silence of the tribe grew big as the cascade. Then her mood suddenly changed: she stopped fondling the child, and began to spank him for having wandered away from the rest. Finally she laughed and laughed, and then began to pet him again.

The old seer turned his eyes on the tremendous landscape and began to talk as if he were in a trance:

"The ducks are hatched in the bulrushes, and

they have scarcely broken through their shells when they throw themselves into the water without having been taught by father or mother. The butterflies burst through their wrappings and wing freely into the sky. The snake comes into being and glides through the weeds with death in its mouth. . . . We were like that, too, and that is why the tribe has been able to survive its sufferings. It is not strange that the child knows how to swim without having been taught. . . . What has happened to us is just that under the domination of another race, we have begun to lose faith in our instincts."

The wild ducks went to their sleeping places on the island. And the Indians took the trail home.

VIII. The Council of the Elders

THE first council of old men was called to take up a very important, though entirely domestic, matter: a quarrel that had divided three families.

They met in the house of one of the elders, signifying that the issue to be discussed was in doubt. It is a custom among the Indians that when the case is fairly plain and the decision therefore not worth much discussion, the council is held in the house of the man to whom justice is due, the one who is obviously in the right.

In some very clear-cut instances, the visit of the old men is itself the decision: the other litigant accepts defeat, and does not even appear to defend his case. The one whose rights have been thus recognized merely serves his visitors a drink of aguardiente or a mug of *atole*.* They talk of things en-

---

* *Atole*—hot, thick drink, made of maize; non-alcoholic. Among the Indians equivalent to our tea or coffee.

tirely alien to the controversy: the good weather, the fine night, or the need for some undertaking having to do with the general welfare. After that, they leave, quite sure that their judgment has been properly understood.

But this time there was no visit to any of the three houses involved in the conflict. They chose, instead, to go to the house of the oldest *huehue*, in respectful recognition of his years and position. He set out small wooden benches for his guests; and, as he went back and forth, attending to their wants, his wide cotton trousers belled around his bare feet. He had a lean face, and his hair was all white. He was the patriarch of the rancheria: he himself had planted the time-scarred plum trees that grew at his door; he had seen the arroyo rise and wash away half the houses; and it was he who had built the little wooden bridge.

There were some who, in comparison with the usual life-span of the Indians, could not be considered elders. But they had been *tequihuis*, tribe officials, and this entitled them to sit in the council. They had been appointed *tequihuis* by the authorities of the district, and in their time they had col-

107

lected the head-tax, had brought the orders for tasks to be carried out, and had jailed many an offender.

There was still another class of men in the rancheria: the braves, who in case of friction with their Indian neighbors, took charge of the war campaigns, but they were not counted among the elders because the hothead interferes with sane judgment.

In one corner of the room which served every purpose—parlor, bedroom, dining-room and kitchen —the women stirred up the fire, supplementing the moonlight that streamed through the door and the cracks of the walls. There was a wide bamboo bedstead in another corner, and across from it a basketwork bin in which the crops were stored when the year was good. Sheaves of the maize that would provide *xinaxli*, the choice seed for the next planting, hung over the fire in the smoke. And, though one could not see them, one could guess that next to the beams of the roof there were two or three fishing poles.

The old men sat in silence. When the contending parties in the conflict arrived, the people of the house went away so that they would not overhear the argument. The three men who came to lay their cases before the council stood at one side of the doorway. One of them told the story in a low voice. His strong features, to which the near-by fire gave the look of an ancient copper medallion, contrasted with the sweetness of his speech.

"This man, my friend," he began to explain, "when my daughter was twelve years old, came to ask for her in marriage for his boy. I do not need to tell you that the son of this friend of mine was healthy, handsome, and a good worker. I could not refuse him my daughter who, as you know, is beautiful and industrious. Therefore I accepted the *tlapalole:* two hens, two measures of beans, a calabash, a handkerchief and a bottle of aguardiente, from which he, his wife, my wife, and I each took a drink, thus sealing the agreement that our children would marry. But they were not able to marry because the boy, as you know, had the misfortune to break his leg when the three whites, who were here looking for gold and medicinal plants, tortured him on the hillside. It is so well known that I need not have mentioned it: that is why we killed the white, that is why we were pursued and why we fled to the forest. . . . The young man still cannot work, and may never be able to. My friend and I agreed to wait because we know that our children love each other, although in accordance with our custom they do not see each other. Unfortunately, time has passed, and the boy can hardly walk. He has shrunk to half his size, with his legs as twisted as dry, burned roots, shriveled like a spider: he who was so strong and beautiful."

The father of the unfortunate boy said, more by nodding his head than in words:

"It is all true."

Then he argued:

"But he will get well. Furthermore, because he is as he is, he needs a mate. You, judges of my tribe, will do him justice, because it was you who sent him as a guide for the whites, who tortured him and threw him down the cliff to his misfortune. I shall work, so long as my son remains ill, for him and for her."

The old men were so still they looked like statues. The three who were taking part in the case looked at one another over their heads.

The father of the girl in dispute went on explaining:

"This is how matters stood when one night this other friend of mine came and said: 'Your daughter will not be able to marry the man to whom she is promised, because he cannot work. How is he going to provide for her? Are you going to support the grandchildren, if you have any? For the sake of your daughter, for his sake, for the sake of their children, they should not marry. Give me the girl as a wife for my son: he is strong and a good worker. Furthermore, tell me, who can match him in hunting? And, as you know, I am not a poor man. . . .' At the time that this other friend was saying these things, he told his wife to give me their *tlapalole:* two hens, two measures of beans, a calabash, a handkerchief, and a bottle of aguardiente. I tried to oppose it, because neither I nor my daughter was free to enter into any other agreement, but he went away, leaving his presents behind him; and now that we are all three here, before you, the elders, I want you to tell me to whom I should return the things that bind the contract: to this one or to that one. My wife is outside with everything that I need to give the *tlapalole* to whomever you indicate. Let experience decide, for I do not want my friends to

111

continue looking with anger upon each other, on account of myself or my daughter. I shall do whatever experience says. . . ."

The old men meditated. One of them went over to stir the fire which was about to go out. The father of the crippled boy spoke:

"Our customs have established that another man's woman is untouchable. Moreover, that the maiden asked for in marriage is sacred, and that neither the one nor the other can be looked at with covetous eyes. How many times have you, my fathers, ordered the punishment of an offender, as in the case of the whites who ran after the girl at the arroyo? My son is in misfortune, it is true, but it is your fault, venerable ones, and he has the right to the daughter of my friend. What, does the wounded pigeon have no mate? If he cannot work, I shall work for him. This man, merely because he is rich among us who are poor, has humiliated my house, disregarding the *tlapalole* of my son! If this is what he was planning, his son should not have told us that my boy was lying wounded at the foot of the mountain. Maybe he saved him from being devoured by the buzzards or wild beasts only in order

112

to collect for it by taking his woman away from him! Why did he not leave him to die in the forest? That way, the bitterness would not be in my mouth now. I ask for justice, *huehues* of my people . . . fathers!"

The way he held his head, thrown back, revealed the indignation of the offended man, more than what he said.

The one he was talking about answered:

"What you have heard, O venerable ones, is the truth, except for the outrage I am accused of. I asked my friend for his daughter, to marry my son, because I think that she deserves a man who can support and defend her. The son of this other friend, now in misfortune, was like mine or better; but now he is not what he was. If the whites had not tortured the boy, I would have gone elsewhere for a daughter-in-law; but the circumstances oblige me to ask you, O venerable ones, do you want to increase the number of orphans left by the last epidemic? You have now heard the three points of the case, and it is for you to decide: I shall obey whatever the elders of my people say. . . ."

The oldest of the old men said:

"In my opinion, this is a most lamentable case. The boy who is in misfortune—through our fault, according to what this comrade says—is entitled to life and the good things it holds. His father is right in defending the heart of his son. But, to make our decision, we must look further, as if we were going along a strange road. What I am about to say will make a victim and lifelong sorrow; that is, unless my brothers, the other elders, decide in some other way. It is better that there should be one and not many victims. The girl should marry the healthy suitor, because he guarantees the family."

All the old men approved with a nod of the head, and no more words were necessary. The girl's father went to the door, and came back with the presents, or their equivalent, that had been given him a long time ago when his daughter was spoken for.

The father of the crippled boy received the symbols of the marriage contract without saying a word: the hens for abundance; the beans for food; the calabash for water signifying rain, rainbow and health; the handkerchief for belongings; and the aguardiente for joy.

In the same silence, he looked at his rival haughtily; then at the old men, and then he stalked out into the night that had now lost its moon.

IX. Fiesta

THE sound of a drum was heard in the canyon that now was a rocky road but during the rains the bed of an arroyo. The sound was the dry, monotonous thump that means war in some tribes. The women and children raced out like fugitives.

First came some men who removed all possible obstacles from the stony road: a tree trunk, the biggest boulders, and the weeds grown up during the dry months. Then the old man who was beating the drum appeared. He struck it mechanically, not paying much attention to the instrument, and his eyes were on the braves behind him who were yelling with glee, stirring one another up.

They were carrying, hoisted on their shoulders, the great mast for the *patlancuahuitl* or *volador*.*

---

* *Volador*—ancient Indian ceremonial and game, described further on in these pages. Literally, the word means flier in Spanish and was applied by the Conquistadores to this spectacle. Its name in Aztec is *patlancuahuitl*. It is a symbolic dramatization of the four winds and the forces of nature.

It had been singled out and chopped down in the thickest part of the forest. This was the compact crowd that was organizing the fiesta: all the able-bodied men, directed by the *topilis*,* bunched together, putting their shoulders to the middle and the ends of the long, straight tree trunk. They were like big dark ants, lugging a stick of wood to their nest.

The monotonous, even pounding of the drums was now growing faster and more resonant, while a hullabaloo went up from the mass of spectators. The procession had come to a difficult place in the road, and the men who were carrying the log faltered, and were in danger of being crushed. Together they struggled to keep on their feet, and finally, panting with fatigue, got past the hazardous spot. The slow, monotonous rhythm, as if marking the pace, was resumed.

The boy who had once been proud and strong and was now a cripple, because he had served the whites who were seeking gold, was at the edge of the rancheria. He was laughing like a child look-

---

* *Topilis*—Indian officials who act as marshals and messengers and make themselves generally useful. Most young men discharge this service for a certain period of time.

117

ing forward to a game; but suddenly his face contracted with pain that was not physical. He had
seen, among those who were yelling the loudest, his
rival, the one who had come upon him in the forest,
and who had taken from him the girl who was to
have been his wife.

Leaning on his rude crutch, or rather dragging
himself after it, he started home. His more crippled leg swung back and forth at each step as if
trying to trip up the other one. His head, firmly set
on a solid neck and muscular shoulders, seemed to
be the only part of him that had been salvaged. It
was like one of those heads on medals and coins,
strong and beautiful, above the misshapen chest.

Every year, before his misfortune, he had gone
with the rest to cut the *volador* in the mountains.
He had taken part in the anxious search among the
highest and straightest trees until the old men had
made up their minds which one to take. Before
the axes were put to use, the tree was consecrated.
The sound of the drum and the *chirimia* began.
The seer spoke to the branches, to stop them from
taking revenge when they were chopped down and
fell like the blows of a heavy hand; to the trunk,

118

so that it might be easy on the dancers who, during the fiesta, would risk their lives on its highest point; and finally, to the roots, to appease their anger at the mutilation.

The *tlachisqui* finished, he poured an offering of aguardiente on the earth, and simultaneously the first ax was swung. The rite was complete. The cripple had always been one of the most enthusiastic. No one, among those his own age, was his match in making the fiesta. Now he saw himself shut out, not only from the preparations, but also from the traditional games and dances. Hence his grief.

Half-hidden in his house, he watched the men who were now carrying the *volador* into the village. They were surrounded by women and children, exclaiming with amazement at the unusual tree: they had never before had such a high *volador*, nor one so straight. He could see his rival among the young men who were shouldering most of the burden. His shirt was tied around his waist, and his machete was slung on a strap from his shoulder. His torso, supple and muscular, was shining with sweat, and his head was bare.

119

Virile as he seemed, how delighted the cripple would have been—in the days when he was not a cripple—to have met him in some lonely place; what a fight they would have had! They would have used their machetes, fencing in that heavy way that looks harmless when both fighters are skillful, but may easily end with a head sliced clean off at one stroke.

They were taking the *volador* to the little plaza. The crowd clamored gaily while the cripple gazed like a spider that scarcely dares stick its head out of its hole. In a little while the drum stopped beating. They had arrived.

．．

Preparations for the fiesta went on all afternoon and that night. The women swept their front yards. Some of the men cleaned up the plaza and the gallery on one side of it where the *tianguis* was usually held. Others decorated the house that would serve as a church with flowers and palms. And about fifty of the braves raised the *volador* mast and prepared it for the most spectacular part of the festival.

The fiesta began in the morning with the consecration of the *volador*. A thick cable, wound around it in loops from the ground to the top, made a kind of ladder. The base of the mast was held steady by heavy spikes used as wedges. At the top there was a large spool to which the cable was fastened. From it hung four planks like a square around the mast. A small stool crowned the structure.

The old *tlachisqui*, now in the rôle of a priest, made a sign to the musicians, and the peculiar melody of the ritual began. The musician performed on a drum and a *chirimia* at the same time; the drum was hung around his neck, and he managed the *chirimia* with one hand. His music attracted the Indians as a bell does bees. The old man bent down at the base of the mast, simulating the act of cutting it down. His prayer was a plea for the protection of the men who were going to dance at the top. He asked the sun not to blind them; the winds not to blow them over, and the spirits of those who had most distinguished themselves on the *volador*, to guard their brothers.

Then he laid the offerings down at the foot of the trunk: eatables and bunches of marigold.

Finally he sprinkled aguardiente on the ground, and drank some himself. The crowd pressed forward to see the beginning of the festival. By now the sun was high. And the *chirimia* and the drum changed their liturgical air for a more lively, almost happy one.

The men who were going to dance made their way through the milling crowd. The first to climb up the mast was a young man with gay bandannas tied on his head and hands and wearing very white cotton trousers and shirt. He bounded up the mast, catching on to the loops of the cable that wound around it like a great snake. When he got to the top, he sat down on the stool and waited for the rest of the dancers.

The second man up was the musician with his drum and *chirimia;* then three more young men. They took their places each on one of the planks of the square, first tying themselves around the waist to the spool with ropes wound on it.

The sound of drum and *chirimia* began. All eyes were on the dancer who sat at the very top and was preparing to stand. When he rose the silence below was so deep that the music seemed to grow louder.

He danced, jumping up and down on a space hardly large enough for the soles of his feet. Keeping time to the music, he bowed toward the four cardinal points, and in the same movement waved his bandanna over the heads of his companions, bending down as if to tell them some secret; then leaped again, each time so high that it looked like certain death. Now and again he let out a whoop, and was answered by the others up there with him.

The dance finished, he sat down on his stool. The brave with the drum and *chirimia* went down the rope ladder, and the dancer took his place on the plank, tying the free end of the rope around his waist. When the music started again from below the four men on the planks dived into space.

As the ropes unwound the spool began to turn. The men in the air whirled in wider and wider circles. With their heads down, and their arms stretched out like the wings of a bird, they seemed the realization of man's age-old desire to fly.

At times they shrieked like eagles, and were answered by the enthusiastic crowd. The music was as fast as the whirling of the fliers. If the dancer had fallen from his stool while he was performing,

123

the others would have tried to catch him in flight, launching themselves into the air in this way.

When they were on the ground again, they were treated to a drink of aguardiente and invited to eat, for they had been fasting, that being the first rite of performers on the *volador*.

A few hours later, the *volador* had become just another game instead of a ceremony. But certainly one of the most exciting. There were other dancers, directed by a man who was shouting and waving a machete, who were performing in front of the house improvised as a church. They wore head-dresses decorated with small mirrors and colored papers. Their torsos were bare and their trousers rolled half-way up the leg. They carried rattles made of dry gourds with pebbles inside, which they shook in time with the music.

The performers faced each other in two parallel rows. Their captain went back and forth between them. They began a dance that is a perfect expression of symmetry: the same steps toward the right, then toward the left. They crossed and changed places and then, at a command from the captain, they all made a half-turn: one row to the left, one row to the right. He used the machete like a baton, but to guide the dancers rather than the music, which was made by a strident violin and guitar.

The crowd had now collected in front of this house. Here the priest * had begun his services, and this attracted them more than the dance, for he came to the rancheria only once a year, and there were many parents with children to baptize and many couples waiting to be married. White was the outstanding feature of the crowd, the white of unbleached cotton cloth and new palm-straw; humble clothing. The new beads on the women's *huipil* † and *quexquemetls* blazed red on the white.

From behind a low stone wall the eyes of the cripple followed one of the couples who were about to be married. The girl, with her hair glossed down over her ears in two waves and pulled smooth at the back of her neck, her embroidered blouse, and her gay-bordered cotton skirt, was more beautiful than ever. She had a calabash bowl in her hands,

* The priest referred to in this case is Catholic, whereas the ceremonies of the consecration of the *volador* were pagan.

† *Huipil*—native tunic blouse made with a single piece of cloth doubled over; the standard garment since long before the coming of the Spaniards, and still in use among most peasant women in Mexico and Central America.

125

as if to catch the tears from her downcast eyes. The man, dressed in white, wore a brand-new straw hat. A red scarf was knotted around his neck, and his light blanket hung over one shoulder.

The cripple looked on from a distance, his eyes filled with grief as deep as the seeming indifference of his people. After several couples had come out, he saw the one he was watching enter. The girl followed her man with short steps, her eyes on the ground.

The scene taking place before the altar must have occupied the cripple's imagination. He did not wait for the couple to emerge, but went home, leaning on his rude crutch. His withered left leg made him look as if he were about to kneel; the thigh and heel almost touched. And it was his best leg; it supported his body. The other, twisted forward, swung around every time the crutch came down on the ground.

In pain from its own bitter poison, the spider was on its way back to its hole, while the others, shouting drunkenly and full of gaiety, danced on.

∴

Everybody was happiest when the *tianguis* was

going on. There were many stands selling cotton cloth and trinkets, but many more selling aguardiente. These attracted customers by letting them sample it free; and in a very short while were overwhelmed by the demand. Any number of persons, especially full grown men, showed signs of intoxication. They talked, they argued, they picked fights. Their traditional muteness had vanished under the action of alcohol. The noisiest and most disorderly were arrested and taken to jail, set up in an old barn; the next day they would be sweeping the streets and the plaza.

The fiesta recapitulated four centuries of painful history: first, the dancing, the music and the *volador* —the ancient ways; then, alcohol and disorder. Some of the men stretched themselves out at the doors of the houses, like swine. They were old *tequihuis* abusing their immunity: they shoved, they brawled, they shed tears, and finally they fell asleep wherever they happened to drop.

By this time the uproar caused by the drinking was so great—even the *topilis*, the tribe officials, were intoxicated—that no one cared any more what was or was not done at the *volador*. At the

127

beginning of the festival, no one was allowed to attempt the dangerous feat who was not in perfect physical condition, and who had not observed the preparatory rites: he must have fasted, asked the gods for protection, and abstained from intercourse with women, at least during the preceding night.

Now, anybody went up who wanted to. The fliers all yelled drunkenly. The one on top had climbed up with suspicious difficulty. The drum and *chirimia* seemed to be tired out, yet no one in authority seemed to realize that the spectacle should be discontinued.

There was a swarm of dark heads, some with new hats, below; above, the man with the red handkerchiefs danced in such a way as to make the blood run cold.

He bowed toward the east; then he paid his respects to the place where the sun was setting. With a leap, he faced southward, and with another, back to the north. The fliers answered his yells with others as harsh.

Suddenly, a howl unlike the rest, one pitched to a key of intense anguish, went up. The man on top had lost his balance, and for a brief moment, his body swayed in the air with the toes of one foot barely touching the stool. He tried to recover himself, but failed, and plunged swiftly down into the deep silence below. One of the *voladores* dived to meet him, attempting to make their trajectories cross; but the unlucky Indian slipped from the flier's hands that were hooked like claws.

He hit the ground with a dull thump, like a ball of mud flattened against a wall. The crowd milled around him. A *tequihui*, so drunk he doubted the man was dead, kept raising and dropping one of the arms. It made a sound like the body of a man who has been struck by lightning: the crunching noise of broken bones.

He had landed flat on his face, spread-eagled. The *tequihui* kept looking for the face, first on one side and then on the other, but could not find it. They would all have laughed if the sight had not been so gruesome: the drunken man had such an idiotic air, and was so full of genuine amazement when it dawned on him that there was no face; just a flat surface.

Screaming, a woman pushed her way through the crowd. She seemed in doubt, and she, also, looked for the dead man's face. Finding none, she examined the stitches on his shirt and looked at the shape of his hands. Her fears were confirmed and again she began to cry out:

"*No tlacatl* . . . my man!"

∴

When the moon rose, dancing to the music of a violin and a harp began in the gallery where the *tianguis* had been held. Torch lamps were burning in the archways. The favorite dances were *xochipitzahua*, or little flower, and the *zacamandu*.*

The women danced demurely, with their eyes down, taking very small steps and holding their embroidered skirts wide, as if they were going to gather a harvest of fruits in them. The men, in their new *huaraches*, stomped heavily; now advancing, now retreating, then going around and around the women, like the cock when courting the hen.

Now and again, a plaintive voice went up in a song that was something like this:

---

* *Zacamandu*—literally, "sheaf." A vigorously rhythmic dance tune, a particular favorite for fiestas.

Xi-quite, cihuatl-cinti
Look, woman slender as the maize,
campa xochitl mo tepana
There where the flowers are in rows,
ni-mo cuepas ayitochi
I shall become an armadillo,
ni-pehuas ni-tlahuahuanas
I shall begin to scratch the earth,
*ni-quisate campa ti-cochi.**
And I shall dig out at the place you sleep.

There was an argument going on in one of the live-liest groups near an aguardiente stand about who was superior on the *volador:* the local performers or their neighbors. Several townsmen of the Indian who had fallen from the *volador* pole and had died such a frightful death, were here. To them it was an affair of honor; there had been many famous dancers-in-the-sky among their ancestors.

Since they all wore machetes hung at their belts— holiday ornaments and signs that the wearers were somebody—tempers flared up quickly. A battle be-

---

* This is an ancient poem, handed down orally by the descendants of the pre-Conquest Aztecs. The language, as throughout the book when Indian words or phrases are used, is Aztec; also known as *nahuatl* or *mexicano.*

gan, and only the miracle of their skill kept it from becoming a general massacre.

For hours the men of the rancheria fought with the visitors, goading one another on with savage yells. They fenced with incredible mastery. Sometimes it looked as if one of the fighters had been struck on the head; but with a magnificent bound, he turned up a short distance away, sharpening his weapon on the stones that flung out fugitive sparks in the darkness.

At daybreak three corpses, with frightfully mangled arms, were found.

X. Fear

I n the dim light of dawn a man emerged from a dark alley. He walked hurriedly, like someone going to get medicine for a person seriously sick in his family.

He was on his way to see the *nectenquetl*, the honeyman, by which name the medicine man was known. He was famous throughout the region, not for his beehives, but for his feared and mysterious witchcraft.

Besides the machete at his belt, his provision sack with his lunch and his *huaraches* tied to the cord of the sack, the man carried the presents with which he would ask for the sorcerer's aid: a hen, some eggs, and a bottle of aguardiente. The fee would be settled when they talked.

The road unfolded in slopes, hollows and drops, in the full light of day. In spite of his age, the man breathed only a little more heavily, as if for relief, at the end of the steepest climb. Whenever he met other travelers, whether he knew them or not, the indispensable greetings were exchanged: a slight brush of the fingertips. He was careful not to give the real reason for his trip, inventing one pretext or another. At the end of a great bend around a hill, he came to a village on an arroyo that flowed almost in the middle of the brush houses, which looked like great heaps of rubbish.

The witch doctor was busy when he arrived, defending his bees in a fierce battle with *tepehua* * ants. He had been out in his field when suddenly he was told that the invaders were detroying his hives.

The fights between bees and *tepehuas* have all the characteristics of ancient struggles between sedentary peoples (the bees) and savage nomadic tribes (the ants). The ants arrive suddenly; climbing in long black lines up the supports of the hives, they penetrate the shelters and give battle. Their object is to sack the settlement, taking the wax and honey.

---

* *Tepehua*—the name of a savage nomad tribe that lived by loot. The ants that are known by this name have that character too. They are dark insects, almost as large and just as fierce as the red ant, but thinner.

134

The bees put up some sort of battle and manage to make some inroads with their stings on the besieging hordes; but the attackers almost always win, unless the owners of the honey factory come to the aid of the workers. Sometimes the bees prefer to abandon their houses and their wealth, setting off on a zooming flight following the queen, while the ants retreat to their caves, taking with them the fruits of their piracy.

This was what the witch doctor was doing, defending his workers who had just been attacked by an army of *tepehuas*. The best weapon is fire: with great torches of brush it is easy to cut into the columns of ants, burning them as they scatter, and to beat back the detachments which have not yet penetrated the hives. The visitor gave valuable help to the medicine man, as did the women of his household, who had quickly rallied to the defense. The ground was covered with cadavers, attackers and defenders indistinguishable.

A small cloud of bees flew from one of the boxes. It was a whole flock, escaping in search of a better home. The witch-man quickly rang a little bell as he followed the swarm, already circling over the near-by trees. The sound captivated the queen who, poised on a very low branch, gathered her subjects around her in a cluster. The witch-man brought a box which had been freshly sprinkled on the inside with rose water. Then with his hands, familiar with bees, he pushed them inside. He took the box to the place where the former home of the fugitives had been. From the abandoned hive he took whitish slabs of wax, studded with cells full of honey.

This was one of the honeyman's principal businesses, for his clients were heavy consumers of wax, in accordance with instructions for the practice of witchcraft. As host he told one of the women to bring a bench, and the two men sat down in the shade of a tree.

Before stating his errand the visitor put his gifts in the hands of the witch doctor. The mere fact that they were accepted meant that the *nectenquetl* would listen. Evidently the help he had received in beating off the ants had disposed him favorably toward the petitioner, for he uncorked the bottle and offered his visitor a drink. For himself, he declined, however, saying he would drink after having finished with the bees, because they hate alcohol, and the mere smell of it infuriates them; whereas without it, they can be handled confidently. Or, he may have feared poison.

The stranger spoke. The medicine man of his village was casting a spell on him in the service of an enemy. He wanted protection with the same weapons that were being used against him. The day before, he had noticed dirt recently turned in the yard of his house. Moved by an impulse of suspicion and fear, rather than out of mere curiosity, he had dug there and found three figures of *cua-amatl*, wood-paper, all pierced with thorns. Besides that, he had also found three eggs painted black and three stalks of marigold, the flower of the dead.

Then he explained the background on which his suspicions were based: a neighbor of his had asked for the hand of a certain girl for his son. But they had never married, because the young man was in no condition to work: some whites had thrown him down a mountain and his legs had been crushed. Since the betrothed couple could not be married, he then asked for the same girl, for his own son. The

137

elders of the rancheria had looked into the case and
the decision had been made in his favor. Neverthe-
less the father of the cripple was angered and had
become his mortal enemy. He concluded:

"It is he who seeks to do me harm."

The witch doctor then asked for a detailed description of the figures he had found. His client
said that one of them had a thorn stuck in its heart,
and another thorn in its head and many in its arms
and legs. This figure was made in one piece to
the feet, while the other two, similarly punctured
with thorns, forked from the crotch.

The witch doctor gave his diagnosis:

"That man who is your enemy is the one who
is trying to harm you. The figure with legs in one
piece is your wife; the two open from the crotch
are yourself and your son. They plan nothing
against the girl, for they hope that when she is
left alone . . ."

"That is why I have come. Give me your protection and turn their evil back on my enemies. You
are strong. Your name travels over the earth, while
I am like one of the ants that we burned. But I
have that with which to pay for your services.

While you are in my house, you shall be treated as is your due!"

The witch doctor accepted. He finished his work with the hives, gave the necessary instructions to his wife, and taking the paraphernalia of his craft, left, followed by his client. As they went along he would stop at times to point out some plant and talk of its curative powers: this one makes women sterile, that one makes them fertile, this one cures madness, the other makes birth pangs easy, and that other causes death. . . . His traveling companion heard him with the respect that an oracle arouses.

∴

The magic work began behind closed doors. The witch doctor lighted four of the candles he had brought; they represented the four members of the family. Those four lives, menaced by their enemies, would last according to the way their corresponding candles burned.

He then lighted three more, but upside down; that is, from the base: one was the rival witch doctor, one was the enemy, and the third was the enemy's son: so that the fires of evil would attack

139

them all over, from head to foot, and increase their suffering. While the candles burned, lighting up the whole house, the witch began to look into the powers of the enemy.

He threw a piece of alum into the fire. In the flames, the salt twisted into a strange shape that, the witch said, was the maimed boy. And, indeed, the figure was like a bust held up by deformed legs. This discovery confirmed all suspicions and now no one had the least doubt. The two women watched wide-eyed from a corner of the room. As the medicine man looked at the strange image, explaining his observations, their amazement grew.

"The witch doctor who helps your enemy is a *nahual*, which means that he has a great deal of power, and is one of those who can, at will, transform himself into anything he pleases. . . . Your enemy is a master fisherman; a great swimmer, and no one knows how to cross the river as he does, swollen though it may be. . . . The boy, the poor cripple, is very sad, and has a whole sea of hate in his soul. . . ."

He pointed out a small hollow, burned in the alum, which he said was the sea of hate made by disaster in the soul of the boy. With his listeners agog, he then turned to a small image on an altar and prayed, buzzing like a big fly: the names of saints could be heard among the invocations to the winds, to the waters, and to the earth.

He took the three punctured figures and slowly pulled out the thorns that had caused so much pain to their living originals. He put them in a little pile; and they all sighed with satisfaction as when an aching tooth is removed. They were even more satisfied when he stopped up the wounds of the dolls with the wax shed in tears by the candles that represented the four lives in the family.

He had, in fact, already begun to check the malady. Now he would turn it back on the enemy. With handfuls of beneficent herbs and tobacco he "cleaned" the two couples, while the best copal of the forest burned in the fire: he wiped them from head to foot, meanwhile mumbling a prayer full of invocations.

The spell had been broken. He then cut three dolls out of the special paper he himself had brought. They were masculine figures, and he began to stick them with the same thorns he had

141

taken out of the others, bringing smiles of angry joy to the faces of his spectators.

He gathered up his paraphernalia, put it in his bag, and on his way out motioned to the two men of the house to follow. The younger hung his machete at his waist; the old man picked up his hat; and the three went out silently into the full-bloomed night.

They stopped at the house of their enemies and listened. There was not a sound; not even the dogs had smelled them; or, perhaps, recognizing that they belonged to the rancheria, they made no sign of hostility. Very cautiously the witch dug with his companion's machete, until he had made a hole about four inches square. He put in it the three paper dolls bristling with thorns, and some other equally sinister objects; sinister, at least, in intention.

The young man covered it all up with part of the upturned earth, carefully smoothing the surface, and took away the rest of it so that their enemies would not discover the evil cache. By the time they were out on the road again, the position of the big stars indicated it was near midnight. The three

Diego Rivera. 36

men hurried to get to the top of the hill chosen for the ceremony.

It was a solitary peak open to all the winds, isolated from other hills that might obstruct the words addressed to the deified forces of nature. At the top, the witch-man quickly took out the things he needed: one of the brightest stars was about to reach its zenith.

He gave the earth food and drink. The aguardiente was sprinkled like dew, and the eatables were laid reverently on a rock. He stationed the two men to the east, and the three candles consecrated to the enemies to the west: for the first, light, sun, and life; for the others, night, the grave of the sun, and death.

He kneeled and began to pray in a monotone:

"Gods of the night who hear me: be gentle to my friends and cruel to my enemies; stars, give light to my brothers and hide your faces from my competitors; father sun, who art about to arrive, lend me all your power so that the wicked shall no longer be able to look upon you; winds, which are the freshness of the earth, lash them; and you, mother earth, spouse of the sun, give me the power

145

to return them evil for evil: let them meet misfortune there where the deer leaps, where the fish swims, where the crow nests, where the snake crawls, where the ant lives, where the eagle shrieks, where the dove coos. . . ."

When they were ready to leave, the witch doctor lighted the three candles that stood for the enemy, upside down as before; and they started down the hill. The three points of light made the earth no less dark, nor did they add to the brightness of the skies.

XI. The Nahual

THE news aroused deep satisfaction rather than sorrow: the witch doctor of the village, who had been especially feared for his powers as a *nahual*,* was dead. At daybreak, word flew from door to door in the rain.

Everybody knew that one of the families in the feud had brought a powerful witch from a distant village, so the death of the local medicine man was attributed to the craft of a stranger. And what a death! They all discussed it, but only those who fully trusted their listeners dared mention its secret cause.

People thought, to themselves, that the dead man

---

* *Nahual*—a supernatural human being who can become any animal at will, assuming its appearance and powers, with special magic of his own besides. Also, a human being whose soul dwells at the same time in some powerful animal. The widespread belief has many variants in American Indian lore. The main idea is of a "loose" or detachable spirit, which can house its powerful magic in many forms. In Mexico it is frequently pictured as a bird with a human head, an image found also in ancient Egypt.

was the first victim of the struggle—the war between the families estranged by the girl whom the two young men desired: one not able to work, the other at the height of his healthy youth.

The fear aroused by the dead *nahual* was a mere shadow of what he had been able to inspire when he was alive. Terrible and mysterious things were attributed to him: to punish a neighbor who stole some ears of maize, he had dried up his hand and shriveled it into something like a misshapen mallet. Another time, paid to take revenge on a family, he had wiped it out completely with a rare disease; even the animals were destroyed.

He had the evil eye: if he looked upon a child that pleased him, it sickened; he then had to purify it with prayers and strange ceremonies, to make it healthy again. If he went through a field, and the vigorous crop stirred his greed, the plants wilted as if scorched by a long drought. But all this was nothing compared to the stories of his dark prowlings and practices. It was remarked that only the night before, the dogs had howled endlessly and, besides, the screech-owl had called, cried rather, near the dead man's house. They were surer than

148

ever that dogs can see things in the dark invisible to human beings, and that the screech-owl heralds death.

Nights like that were nights of dread, when dogs and owls break the silence of the rancherias. Children cling to their mothers, shaking with fear; the women clasp their men's hands, and the men listen, ears pitched to the mysterious voices of the night in futile anxiety to penetrate the meaning beyond the blurred phenomena of the shadows. Why was it that on nights like these the dogs did not bark in the same way as when they faced a jaguar, or when they chased a buck, but in a frightening way, always ready to cower in the most protected corner of the house? Why was it that on such nights the owl's hoot was not, as usual, husky and friendly, but as if it were laughing and crying in turn?

But all this was nothing to what had now happened. The witch doctor lay dead in his own bamboo bed, but there were bruises and lesions all over his body, as if he had gone through all the brambles in the sierra, or had been clawed by an entire pack. Since the whole village knew how he spent

149

his nights, they thought they could all guess what this meant.

He was known to be a *nahual*. Everybody said that when the rancheria was quiet under the weight of the darkest nights, he would turn himself into a jaguar, a bear, or an enormous serpent, to go growling unmolested through the fields and ranches, stealing the most valuable things he found. That is why there was always plenty of meat and grain in his house.

Sure that these things were all true, his neighbors would tell how he shut himself up in his house and uttered mysterious words, threw copal in the fire, and then jumped on the hearthstones, in a cloud of smoke, emerging transformed into the beast whose shape he had previously chosen, ready to bring back a fat hog or a dozen stolen hens in his jaws.

His wife then would have to go through the ritual that would restore him to human form when he returned. A still more terrible story was told of his father: they said that his wife, weary of being mistreated, or else attracted to another man perhaps, had refused to turn him into a man again at

150

the end of his run one night. Since the ritual requires that the transformation be made before daybreak, the *nahual* scratched at the door of his house
till sunrise, begging for entry. But the streets
grew gradually lighter and his memory faded, as
if all the departing shadows were entering his head.
And thus, alien to his whole past, he fled to the
mountains in the form of a strangely spotted leop-
ard. They say he was found dead by some hunters:
his face half animal, half human, and his hair so
long it came to his shoulders.

And now his son, a *nahual* too and the heir to his
strange knowledge, had died in his own bed. The
people who knew most said very guardedly that the
witch doctor was caught during one of his runs, or
that he might have met with some stronger *nahual*,
or had fallen into a trap and been chewed up by
the dogs until they instinctively smelled the truth
and let him go.

Wounded and with empty jaws, he must have
run home through the brambles. His wife just
managed to bring him back to human shape;
and there he was, on the bamboo mat, smeared
with blood and covered with wounds, some like

thorn scratches, and others like slashes of dogs' fangs.

The witch from the other village must be very powerful, they said, if he could cause the death of a *nahual*.

Here was another being struck down in the kind of war that had been going on for centuries of superstition—a family feud that would be handed down like a legacy of hate.

XII. Yoloxochitl

THE famous honeyman, the witch from the other village, who had recently enlarged his fame with the death of his rival, the *nahual*, was now being called in again. This time he was needed to cure the young woman who by decree of the elders had married the man who could work for her, rather than her first betrothed whom she loved.

She was not the same girl any more. She who had been firm-fleshed and had walked lightly as a doe just before its mating season, now was ailing, and when asked why she was so sad, she would put her hand up to her breast and say it hurt. She spent most of the time in a corner of her house, mechanically performing her quiet tasks.

People had begun to say she was the one who had been affected by the evil spells that the *nahual* had cast at her husband and his family. The witch doctor thought for a long time after hearing about

153

it. Finally, he decided to speak, confirming, though hesitantly, the suspicion that witchcraft was causing her illness. But before he prescribed a remedy he decided to make an examination; not of the sick body, but among the mysteries of his craft.

He lighted the fire and threw copal into it, filling the house with a pleasant aroma. Then, as before, he put a lump of alum in the coals. The transformation was immediate: the heat made the alum expand, and by some odd circumstance it took on the form of a heart.

As he studied the alum, he began to talk:

"It often happens that a spell directed at someone who has a strong spirit is deflected and strikes a member of his family; or, very often, an animal, nearly always the most cherished one; for example, the dog who always trails his master."

He called the family over to look at the peculiar shape of the alum:

"Look! The sickness is in the heart. It is only because she is young that she has been able to resist it. Your enemies attacked the very source of life. It was surely that big thorn I pulled out of one of the paper figures that caused this illness, though

154

it was not aimed at her. But she will recover. . . ."

Then, with the gravity of a priest, he very deliberately went and sat down on a wooden bench. He seemed perturbed. He asked his host for a drink of aguardiente; sipped it, and began to talk haltingly, as if remembering something with great difficulty:

"Once upon a time there was a beautiful girl, almost a princess, daughter of a powerful chief, who also had a pain in her breast. The old men say she was so beautiful that when she passed along the roads the flowers bowed to her; when she went out to her gardens, the birds forgot to sing, they were so entranced; and at night, the stars would cling like flowers on the branches of the lemon trees in order to give her better light. The girl loved one of the young warriors who was a subject of her father's. He was matchless in battle; no one could dance on the *volador* like him; and he was so gallant and so beautiful that all the women blushed when they looked at him. But another chief, more powerful than the father of this princess, asked her hand for his son. She did not even dare to explain that she loved a man of her

155

own people. As a daughter obedient to the discipline of her family tradition, she accepted the marriage without protest, and more especially as the old chief remarked happily that the alliance of the two domains would bring many benefits. For, joined, the two could undertake the conquest of the barbarous peoples who lived in the lands where the sun went down. They celebrated the wedding for a whole moon. When the new moon rose, the princess was taken away by her husband, borne on the shoulders of four distinguished warriors. But in a short while she fell ill. They brought her the richest dishes and the most delicate blossoms, but she only sighed, and said that she had a pain in her heart; and, still sighing, she died the night when the first moon of her absence was full. Her husband mourned a great deal for her. His subjects all wept with him. And, where she was buried, a strange plant sprouted. A flower equally strange bloomed on it, shaped like a heart, and so they named it *yoloxochitl*, the flower of the heart.

"The chief called in the most famous wise men to say what flower this was that no one had ever seen before. They thought the plant represented love, which they all called *tlazotlaliste*, the sickness of attachment, the fever of affection. The old chief and his guards then left them, but all the old men remained looking at the strange plant. They looked and pondered deeply. Finally the oldest discovered the secret that has come down to us like a thread of water trickling in the crack between great rocks: 'If one takes out the brain of a snake to cure its own venom, and if at the foot of each poisonous herb there is to be found its counter-poison, it is logical that the *yoloxochitl*, flower of the heart, should be good to cure illness of the heart.' . . ."

The young husband of the girl, the hunter by profession, who had found his enemy dying in the forest after being tortured by the whites, barely waited to hear the last words of the medicine man. He slung on his machete and went striding away from the house to search in the thickest woods, in the deepest valleys, and on the highest hills, for the flower of the heart.

The medicine prescribed by the witch, found at last in the deepest part of the forest, was taking effect very slowly. The girl, though she no longer

157

complained as before, still kept putting her hand to her breast, as if the slightest movement fatigued her.

The *yoloxochitl* had been dug up, root and all, and was planted next to the house. They took such exquisite care of it that not even its tenderest buds dried. On each twig there was a flower; or rather, a heart. The young woman took one of the buds every morning, and when she did her husband would remember the legend of the princess.

But she was still in danger and her recovery was doubtful. So her husband's father decided to take the case to the council of elders. He was a prominent man, and it was easy for him to call the *huehues* together. On the day of the meeting, his house breathed cleanliness: the yard and the entrance were thoroughly sprinkled and swept; plenty of seats had been provided inside for the visitors; there was a big olla with the victuals of hospitality on the fire; and on a white wooden shelf a dark bottle of aguardiente.

They were all punctual. They sat like bronze statues dressed in white on short sections of logs, waiting for the case to be put before them. Their host began by offering them leaf tobacco which he said he had kept fresh in banana leaves, and that it came from the plants he grew in a corner of his field, near the water, so they could be irrigated when it did not rain.

The old men each pulled up a trouser leg and rolled the tobacco on his bare knee, while the host went from one to the other, giving them a light with the glowing end of a stick. They commented on the quality of the tobacco, while the aguardiente was being passed. The bottle went from hand to hand, beginning with the oldest and ending with the youngest.

Finally the host put his problem before them, first apologizing for taking the liberty of calling them together at his house. He reminded them of the girl's story and of how she had been disputed between his son and the cripple. He recalled the decision they had once made in his favor. But, he added, his rival was not satisfied with the judgment and had declared war upon him; he had cast a spell, but the spell had not affected him, nor his son, nor his woman; only the girl, who now had a pain in her heart; it came from a thorn that the witch

159

doctor, hired by his enemy, thrust into a paper doll, as if into the flesh itself.

He finished and asked that the man be punished. But as soon as they heard that the affair had to do with witchcraft, the elders rose and remained standing while they listened to the rest of the complaint. Then the oldest of the elders spoke for them: they could not pass judgment on such a case as this; their experience, great as it was, could not take in all truth. If it had been a question of a piece of land in dispute, a contested hen, or of a fight, that is what they were for, to do justice; but witchcraft . . .

It was the ancient fear of that which is beyond understanding. And the old men slipped away, their wide cotton trousers swinging back and forth over their bare feet as they walked.

XIII. The Man of the Forest

THE *cuatitlacatl*, man of the forest, had come home after having been gone two weeks. During this time he had been doing the kind of work he liked least: cutting wood for a mestizo's sugar mill, finding pasture for the teams used in the harvest, and interminably tending fires.

For himself, because he disliked agriculture, he neither sowed nor reaped; there was reason for him to be called man of the forest. When the rest went to clear the earth for the planting, he went hunting in the woods with his dogs. And, while the others were harvesting, and filling their granaries, he sold pelts and bartered meat for the staple foods of his people.

He had another important source of income, as *coatenquetl*, snake owner. This meant that whenever anybody needed a deer snake, named so because its jaws resembled a buck's, to clear a field of gophers, rats, and all kinds of pests, the man of the forest could supply it.

The deer snake is large and strong, but not venomous. It is so easily tamed that it often lives, inoffensive and amiable, inside the Indians' houses.

Whenever the man of the forest heard that somebody had seen one, he went after it. He began to scout and, after careful observation, prepared to trap the snake. Next he left some creature large enough to produce lethargy, where the snake would find it. After that all he had to do was to pick up the reptile and take it home. Then came the real job: training it. He would whistle in a peculiar way, and then feed it, necessarily something alive.

The villagers rented the snakes from the hunter regularly to destroy the rodents that attacked their ripening crops.

The deer snake would be left in the field, where it waged a patient war. But, to keep it in that one field the owner of the crop would have to take presents to it often. It would drag itself, at the whistle of its master, rolling and heaving, after him.

As a rule, the woodsman had several of these snakes rented out at a time. The pay, nearly always, was a laying hen or a shoat, or a few measures of maize or beans. When the hunter turned his rat-exterminators over to the renters he warned them to treat them well, because, tame as they seemed, if they were angered they became a real danger, even to him. But what he particularly warned them against was going near the snake when they had drunk aguardiente, because the reptile would be very much irritated at the mere odor of alcohol.

It had happened once that an Indian had hired a deer snake for his field, a snake as thick as a man's leg, and so long that it could easily have crushed a wildcat in its coils. The pests disappeared quickly. The gopher holes, from disuse, began to get cluttered with rubbish. Even in the afternoons when rain threatened, and there is always great uneasiness in everything wild, the rodents did not show the slightest signs of life. The snake had done a good job.

When the owner of the field was sure that there was no more work for it, he prepared to return the snake to its owner. Familiar with it by now, it was easy for him, after giving the reptile some favorite titbit, to put it in a huge basket, which was then covered with a cloth.

He started for the rancheria with the valuable cargo on his back. The snake was so heavy that he had to stop and rest several times on the slope. When he came to a refreshment stand, one of those on the edge of the road that are like forced stopping places for every traveler, he put his load down on a bench and went over to the little window to have an aguardiente. Reminded of the warning of the owner, he threw a glance in the direction of the snake. What could it do, being, as it was, a prisoner; and furthermore, now that there was a friendliness almost intimate between them? Self-confidently the man took another drink.

Cheered, but not so careful as before, he shouldered his burden. But he had barely started again when the snake got restless. With a violent thrust it threw aside the cloth that covered the basket; its great jaw struck the man at the back of the neck, knocking him down. Then it began to maul him in the same violent way as an enraged dog picks up a cat and beats it against the ground.

Except this once, the snake renter made out very well. His customers behaved themselves properly, and paid the rent with all due formality.

But at times he had to give up his favorite activities in the forest. This happened whenever the *topilis* brought him orders to serve his turn in the houses of the town functionaries or in the haciendas. This particular time, forced to take the miserable wage usually paid, he was resentful and impatient, especially since he had heard nothing of his wife, whom he had left still sick in spite of the first treatments with the heart-flower.

But the news that she was a little better, plus the offer of a shotgun as pay for his second week's labor, made things easier. The hunter thought about it constantly, because for the first time he would be able to increase his own strength and cunning with the powerful aid of a firearm.

He went back to the village with a thousand plans in his head, caressing the weapon that hung jauntily on his shoulder: with the gun, the machete and the dogs, he could now hunt not only deer and peccary, but even the wildcat and the jaguar. He almost pranced with this war-like

165

thought: if her enemies and their kinsmen persisted in doing him harm through witch doctors, he might settle that too with a shower of bullets!

Even with no more hunting equipment than the little he had now, the same as his father had when he also was young and lived in the forest, what secret could escape him once he learned to handle a shotgun skillfully? Even now no one could match him at hiding traps in the game trails: those traps into which beasts fall on their way to the waterholes or the growing crops—a deep hole, a rudimentary combination of balance between the weight of the animal and the covering above loaded with stones. The animal steps on one of the supports, and the whole thing caves in on him at once. It is weighted according to whatever animal it is set for.

But more than anything else he liked to hunt with dogs, preferably on cloudy days, because then they hold out a long time, until they tire the deer. This was why immediately when he got home and inquired after the health of his wife, he began to look his dogs over carefully, patting them affectionately while they leaped around him like delighted children.

The mother, the old man, and the wife examined very curiously his new acquisition: the shotgun earned with a week of work. He had received, besides, a pouch made of fox-pelt; and in it, a supply of powder, shot and caps. And at the same time he had been shown how to use the gun.

In the evening the family followed its normal routine. The old man wove a small rush basket by the light of a pitch-pine torch and the fire at which the hunter's wife, ill as she was, cooked supper. The old woman made yarn embroidery on a *huipil*. And the young hunter cleaned his gun. They were all silent, each busy with his own thoughts.

With a rag tied to the end of a leather thong, the young man cleaned and cleaned the inside of the barrel. He put it up to one eye; then with the mistrust of a gunsmith he blew into it. The whistle of air through the opening proved its cleanliness. Finally, very carefully, as was proper for a beginner, he put in the cap and let the hammer come down very slowly.

During this operation the dogs watched him in an almost human way. There were three of these apparently worthless, long-snouted, cock-eared Indian dogs, whose endurance matches that of their closest relatives, the *tepechiches*, wild mountain dogs: tenacious black hunters with white collars, who can run all day behind a deer and bring it down to devour a piece of gut only.

The two men pulled their stools near the fire and began to eat their supper. The girl, sitting on the floor, patted tortillas and laid them out smoothly on the *comal*.* The old woman helped with the preparations for the scanty meal, bringing the water gourd and the cocoanut shell containing the salt.

The dogs had also come closer, eying the two men as intently as when the younger was cleaning his gun. Every time someone threw them a piece of tortilla—the leftover of a mouthful—their alert rigidity suddenly melted, then froze again, transforming them back into figures like sculptures.

The supper consisted of beans in a plate held on the knee, a little chili, a pinch of salt, a fragrant herb, and the hot tortillas. When they

---

* *Comal*—large, flat griddle, usually of clay; sometimes iron or tin.

were through, the two men went to get some air.

The girl, tired perhaps from squatting on the floor, got up, holding one hand to her breast as if the pain had not yet disappeared. When she stood, her pregnancy was fully apparent, so far advanced that her thick skirt was lifted in front, exposing her bare feet and ankles.

∴

Bareheaded, barelegged, and breathing deeply, the *cuatitlacatl* went into the forest, followed by his dogs, heading for places where he could hunt unrestricted.

He had his shotgun on his shoulder: blackened steel obviously not much good. The pouch hung on a dark strap across his chest. There was a short machete at his belt; a long one would be a hindrance in the brush.

The dogs, so lean they looked as if they were made of bamboo, stopped frequently to sniff at the bushes. Anyone who has never seen Indian dogs on the trail would never suspect their tenacity and endurance. They do not behave like setters following the deer almost at a walk, and thus without tiring either pursuer or pursued. All that the blooded hunting dog wants is to keep the trail; he follows his prey calmly. The animal runs, then stops to listen; if its enemy comes close, it starts off again; then it stops once more, raising one hoof with which, according to the hunters' tales, it listens. The chase is enough for the setter; the rest, killing the game, it leaves to its master.

But these dogs of the *cuatitlacatl*, like all Indian dogs, were the kind that run at full speed all day without resting, until they wear out the deer and throw it down. They do not depend on their master's shotgun, but on their own strength, like that of their brothers, the wild mountain dogs, not yet shaped to the human will.

At the edge of an arroyo, where the earth was damp and soft, the hunter found fresh deer tracks. The long, sharp marks could not be confused with those of any other split-hoofed animals; they were like twin leaves fixed on the ground. The hunter picked up the trail while his dogs were already ahead, wagging their tails as a sign that they had smelled something. The hoofprints disappeared among some rocks and then showed up again on a slope where the animal had slipped, making long streaks. The dogs raced off into the undergrowth, fighting for the lead.

The hunter was all ears. He slipped his gun off his shoulder. There was a long, nervous howl. One of the dogs had raised the deer in its hiding-place. After that two dogs barked, then the whole pack joined in, clamoring loudly.

The Indian ran along a dry arroyo bed and then waited in a hollow through which the deer generally ran when there was a drive. The Indian heard the dry thump that meant the animal was racing toward him. But the deer sensed him a short distance away and changed its course, making for the lowlands.

The hunter stared at the sky through an open place in the trees. It was cloudy, promising a long run: the dogs could easily circle the plains twice and return to the sierra. With a strong sun the drive would have to end at noon. Now the barking could be heard very far below. The hunter climbed to a high place, and began to shout to his dogs, encouraging them. They got farther away every minute. They did not bay deeply like fine dogs; but yelped in a shrill, nervous way, as if already snapping at the flanks of the quarry.

For a long while nothing was heard. The hunter started off down the slope, running along the trails familiar to him. Renewed yelping made him stop and listen. The noise of the dogs was getting louder; they were nearer. The deer was returning to its favorite haunts, still trying to shake off its pursuers.

The Indian sought out the place where the deer would have to pass. The pounding of its hoofs could again be heard. He caught the barely perceptible breaking of a dry branch. Quickly he placed himself so that he merged with a tree trunk that had been burned in the last forest fire. The buck, its head bowed by the weight of the huge antlers, went by nimbly a few yards away, dodging through reeds and bushes.

The Indian aimed, and pulled the trigger. But the cap did not go off, and the precious opportunity to end the hunt was lost. Soon afterward the dogs passed by, panting as if desperate at not being able to catch their prey.

172

Pursued and pursuers circled the hills. The sun was beginning to push through the clouds, and it was getting hotter and hotter. The hunter waited to see how the chase would come out. The deer described a wide arc and again sped in the direction of the valley. This time it surely would not come back; other failures told him that. So, yelling at the dogs to encourage them, he ran downhill, resolved to enter the territory of the haciendas, though he knew well enough that it was forbidden ground.

It was now noon and the sun was intense. The deer, still unable to get rid of its pursuers, fled for safety into a wide lagoon edged with thick vegetation. The buck plunged in and, because of fatigue, swam clumsily to a bend. Even there the dogs followed to attack.

The hunter arrived just when several men, headed by an overseer, approached. They had stopped work when they heard the dogs bark, to go see whether they could get the deer for themselves. The buck rested for a moment and then again tried to escape, but they blocked every possible way out, yelling and hooting wildly.

173

The hunter jumped into the water. Swimming silently, he came nearer and nearer. When he was a few yards away from the animal he dived. Under water he seized the hoofs of the buck and pulled him down. Then, with the animal momentarily confused, he jumped on its head, grabbed the horns and twisted the great head down into the water, holding it there until there were no more bubbles coming to the surface.

He pulled the buck ashore: sturdy neck, rounded haunch, slender shanks. The dogs, still tired, tongued the moist places around its mouth as if wanting to sink their teeth in. The hunter forgot he was in forbidden territory and felt proud of himself. But the men from the hacienda made him realize where he was. The overseer who was with them betrayed his state of mind plainly in the way he eyed the dead deer.

The Indian began to explain humbly that the buck had been raised by the dogs outside the hacienda, in the sierra. This was an effort to excuse himself for having entered the master's land. But the overseer replied that he was not interested in explanations: the deer had fallen within the property lines of the master, and everything that was in that territory belonged to him.

It took a good deal of pleading before the over-seer was satisfied merely with the best portions: the two hind quarters.

The hunter then began to skin the buck's legs with a knife. As he removed the hide, the rosy flesh appeared, still warm, covered with fat at the loins.

While the Indian worked, throwing a bloody scrap to the dogs now and then, the mestizo lec-tured him ceaselessly: that he must not enter the lands of the master again, because next time his dogs would either be riddled with bullets or he would have to forfeit all the game. The Indian promised not to do it again.

Perhaps to stir sympathy in the overseer, the Indian began to tell him how, not long ago, the peccaries had killed his best dog. In spite of every effort to save him, he had failed, and he felt it as deeply as if it had been a brother, for the dog had served him well. For that reason he buried him carefully, and had put a hundred pennies in a handkerchief which he tied around the dog's neck

175

so he could buy his tortillas on the road to the other life.

The hunter was now in the woods on his way back to the rancheria, following the familiar trails, putting his bare feet down on the soft black earth where there were already other tracks, some split and some broad.

The Indian was carrying the butchered buck on his shoulders. The huge-horned head, tied down by a rope, seemed to be licking its left flank. The tail was like a spear of cane, waving point downward. The dogs followed along gaily. Occasionally they would sniff at the bushes, perhaps smelling some other animal near by. They trotted along in the footsteps of the hunter, stopping to lick up the blood which fell in round red beads on the tender green of the fern.

The man walked bowed under the weight of his burden. He stopped now and then, sweating, blowing hard for relief. The path was like a snake through the forest, undulating and black. In the heat, everything seemed to be torpid: that deep silence when it is hard to tell if the throbbing is in one's own temples or in the mountain.

Suddenly, from the brush a few steps away, came the peculiar grunt of the peccary, something like a hollow thump on a stretched hide. That sound is why the animal is called *tamborcillo*, little drum. The dogs answered with a rush to the thickets.

Beyond, could be heard the clamor of a hundred drums beating furiously, as if calling to battle. It was a whole herd of wild hogs, searching perhaps for woods with more forage. Some of the full-grown peccaries were already pushing their stupid heads through the bushes, charging the dogs, while the latter, their hair standing on end along their spines, and their teeth bared, retreated from the attack.

Conscious of danger, the hunter threw down his burden and got ready to fire at the first and best opportunity, sure that the smell of smoke would frighten the herd. One male, whose great white tusks were like stiff mustaches, came out of the brambles and rushed at one of the dogs.

The Indian fired and the peccary plunged headlong, plowing up the dirt with his snout and grunting like a hog, wallowing furiously in the mud. Perhaps that dying voice was understood by the rest,

177

because the stampede that the shot had provoked stopped suddenly. But the herd turned back and again threw itself on the hunter and his dogs. With speed incredible in such short-legged beasts, the peccaries zigzagged furiously. They do not wound head-on, but attack at a tangent; the tusk, as they pass, neatly slices the flank of a dog or the leg of a man.

The hunter could not get his single-shot weapon reloaded. The number of peccaries was overwhelming; so he retreated quickly. He had already jumped up on the trunk of a tree to put himself out of reach, when the yelp of one of his dogs brought him back to the ground, machete in hand.

He could not desert his whelps. One of them, seriously wounded, was dragging itself, whining, after him. In the position of a warrior—one foot forward and the other back for the retreating jump —he brandished his weapon over the bristling hog backs that passed swiftly within his reach.

The whole underbrush moved, agitated by the fury of the peccaries, revealing their number. The roar of the *tamborcillos* echoed through the forest. At the other end of the hollow the cries of the young

ones could be heard, huddled out of the way, perhaps, as the cattle do with their calves when they
sense the approach of the jaguar.

Though practically surrounded, the hunter was
determined he would not give up the small territory he dominated, so small it could be measured
by the combined length of his arm and machete.
The wounded dog crouched between the man's feet
in the middle of this stronghold.

The other dogs were bulwarked behind a thick
growth of reeds, and they kept poking their heads
and shoulders out when the attack of the peccaries
slowed up a little. The angry tusks slashed deeply
the tender stalks of the reeds.

One crafty hog edged past the place held by the
bravest dog. Deceived by the apparent timidity of
the peccary, the dog came out from behind his de-
fenses. Another hog quickly cut off his retreat,
leaving him trapped between his two adversaries.
In a flash, they both ripped into him. He died
with a long drawn howl that suddenly stopped.

This victory aroused the herd even more. The
hunter realized that his means of defense were di-
minishing, for the dog between his feet was more of

a hindrance than a help; another was already dead, and the third, though more or less secure behind its parapet of reeds, did nothing but bark at a pitch that betrayed its fear.

Once when the avalanche swept in on him, he managed to force it back and then made a dash for a tree, carrying the wounded dog in his arms. But before he reached the nearest trunk, a tusk caught him in the calf.

The leg doubled sharply under him. He kept on trying to jump; straining, while he still had the will to try once more, he felt another blow, and then many more. The hogs shot past, apparently only brushing his flesh, but always running their tusks through it. Finally, realizing the futility of trying to climb, he put the wounded dog down and remained squatted, unable to rise. In that position, he still used the machete for a long time.

The attack grew even more violent: he was struck on the side, on the back, in front; and each blow was a wound. They tormented him like horseflies stinging a cow that keeps on defending herself.

The short machete was becoming entirely ineffectual. In the end, the hunter fell to the ground next to the wounded dog. The herd threw itself on them, grunting.

Their rage quenched, the peccaries started off again. They pushed the boar killed at the beginning of the fight along with their snouts, as they generally do unless panic makes them abandon their wounded or dead. They seem to try to revive them or take them to some hiding-place. But when they have gone in this way for some distance, they end almost always by burying their fangs in the carcass, devouring their own kind.

That night the old man traced his son by the howls of the only dog that had escaped.

∴

The father of the hunter told the story of the tragedy in the mountains as he imagined it must have happened. He held obstinately that it was all a matter of bad luck, determined to get the other, the detestable, version of it out of people's minds.

For witchcraft was stirring a new uneasiness in them. Every person who saw the body of the hunter, covered with wounds, maintained that they were not made by peccary tusks at all, but were

183

the marks of the *tlahuelilo*, the devil himself, which the spirit of the *nahual* now inhabited, and from whom they had all been expecting reprisals.

They said that he only, with his great power, could have surrounded the hunter in the middle of the forest. How could the eyes of the *cuatitlacatl*, so sharp he was able to outmaneuver a deer, fail to notice a whole herd of peccaries and so reach a tree in plenty of time? How was it that his sense of smell, keener than a dog's, did not warn him of their presence? How had his ears been closed to the noise of the herd in motion, when they were so sensitive that they could detect the sound of a snake slipping through the water? In their minds there was not the slightest doubt: the spirit of the man who had died in animal form wandered through the forest, taking vengeance on his enemies.

So now, with the same impelling fear that makes a man put a heavy prop against his door, copal was being burned every night in every house of the rancheria, to ward off the dreaded spirit.

XIV. The River Takes Toll

A MESSENGER was lost. So by order of the precinct judge, about a hundred men, Indian and mestizo land workers, were going down the river looking for him. He was the father of the boy who had been crippled by the exploring whites, and who was now carrying on a fierce feud with his neighbor by means of witchcraft.

They were sure he must have been drowned, for he had not been seen anywhere on the other side. The last news of him came from the couple who lived in the little ranch on the bluff, overlooking the river ford.

The Indian had arrived at the ranch when the sun was fairly high. While he had a drink of *caña* * he had told them where he was going. It seemed the municipal president was using him as a courier

---

* *Caña*—literally, cane; cheap sugar-cane brandy.

185

during his regular shift in town, to carry some very urgent letters to another town. Aged as he was, they chose him because his ability to cross swollen rivers was well known. No one was so skillful as he at managing the *acuahuitl*, a log of balsa wood which the peasants used to cross rivers, riding it as if it were a horse.

The ranch-dwellers advised him to wait for the river to go down a little, because at the time it was very high. But the Indian smiled disdainfully, and said he had been ordered to return the same day. As he spoke, he looked at his ally, the log, leaning up against the fence.

When he had emptied his glass, he slapped his chest which burned from the fiery liquor, and prepared to leave. The owner of the little house stopped him a moment and asked him to bring some things from the town: tobacco and gunpowder; his wife ordered salt and soap.

With the log on his shoulders the man went down the slope to the river, which had risen so high that it flowed in absolute silence: as the peasants say, it was a tight-rope. He tied his shirt, the bag in which he had the important letters, his lunch, and the

186

money for the articles ordered, around the crown of his hat. Then he rolled up his trousers to his loins. From around his waist he took a rope which he made into a kind of bridle for his wooden horse.

Ready, he pushed himself into the muddy stream, still carrying the log. With it on his shoulder, he looked like a man about to be martyred, carrying part of a cross. When he was up to his waist in the water, he went down on his belly against one end of the log, got the other end straight in the swift current, and began to swim.

He held the "bridle" in his left hand, keeping the head of the "horse" always against the current, while with his right arm and his legs he pushed himself along skillfully. To cross directly was impossible, and no swimmer could be expected to do it; but with the help of the log, the force of the water is lessened and the swimmer's strength conserved.

The man bobbed up and down in the tumbling waters, pitching and rocking but always gaining distance. From the cliff, the man and woman of the hut watched him, cheering him on with yells at the most difficult points.

About five hundred yards down his hat appeared

and disappeared intermittently in the rolling waters. They saw him reach the other side finally, and climb up the bank with the log on his shoulder. The woman went inside, sighing with satisfaction at how the Indian had won in his struggle with the river. The man stood there, looking with expressionless eyes at the savagely beautiful landscape, in which the swimmer had now become something of no interest whatsoever. He saw him hide the log among the reeds, put on his *huaraches*, and start off again down the road.

For hours after that the woman sang mournfully and monotonously as she did her work in the house. The man, seated on a rock at the edge of the cliff, smoked impassively while he watched the waters go by, or followed the flight of the cranes and the ducks with his eyes. Tiring of that, he got out his ax and began to chop wood.

His wife had called him to eat; and, between mouthfuls, he remarked that the courier must be reaching the town by now. Afterward, looking at the horizon, he told his wife there was a storm in the sierra. The sky was the color of a burro's belly, and muffled thunder could be heard far away.

These things aroused some fear for the courier, who had not yet returned. The man went down to the edge of the river two or three times to look at a mark he had put on a stone in the morning. He came back each time to say that the river was still rising. Later on in the afternoon he threw himself down to sleep on a bench in the yard.

At the end of the day, a light shower was falling with the sun still shining—"the debtors were paying," as the peasants say of such contradictions. The woman went to bring in her wash, and at the same time she took a look at the stream. The rock her husband had marked was covered completely. The water was now the color of copper, and soon tree trunks began to appear, tossing on the surface.

There was a shout from the other side. Husband and wife went to the edge of the bluff. The Indian was returning. They saw him take his wooden "horse" from among the reeds, remove his shirt, tie his things to his hat, and advance into the river with the log on his shoulder.

The couple, gauging the danger, called to him and signaled with their arms to tell him not to try the crossing. But the orders he had must have car-

189

ried more weight: the messenger went in anyhow.

He might have won out, as before, for he was already in the middle of the stream, though much below the crossing, when there was a sound as if a dam up the river had burst. Trunks and great boughs began to sweep past in greater and greater number. The river seemed to be taking a whole forest with it.

The man was trying vainly to cut through the water faster, striking out with his arms and legs, when one of the big logs hit him. After that they knew nothing of him.

∵

The searching party was looking painstakingly in every bend, every arm, every backwater, for several kilometers down. Their eyes, skilled at reading distances, had turned everywhere for traces of the drowned man. They thought of a number of things that might have happened: that the current had carried him a long way, perhaps even to the sea; that the corpse might by now be in the cave of an alligator, and that these beasts, attracted by putrefying flesh, were making a feast of it; or, perhaps, it might be somewhere deep down, covered with slime.

They had their eyes fixed especially on the best allies in such situations: the buzzards. They followed the flight of these birds with intense interest because it might be that the dead man would be found where they swooped.

Some soared, apparently aimlessly, as if just to exercise their wings, so as not to forget how to fly. Others glided down to the river's edge, to devour some small dead fish.

But every new clue was another disappointment. The sun lighted the backwaters to the bottom, where the sand glistened, newly washed in by the flood as if placer-mining for golden grains.

On both banks, in the shade of the trees, groups of men clustered around fires. Indians and mestizos warmed up their food and ate peaceably, some talking desultorily and others staring at the river. The Indians were of the latter: and none of them remarked that it seemed to be always one of their people who was the victim of fate. Their eyes never left the river. At most they went a few steps from the water to cut wild guavas among the rocks.

191

The mestizos, however, smoked and talked constantly. It seemed they were just carrying out orders, but were not themselves affected by the accident.

One old man with a yellowed gray beard was telling a story. "She was a woman," he said, "very much off on the wrong foot, one of those who like to provoke their husbands by doing always just the opposite of what they are told. She was so given to contradiction that, when her man smacked her behind with his machete, saying, 'To teach you not to do it again, *maldita*,' she would beg him to go on hitting her, saying it was a pleasure. Well, the old woman was drowned, and the neighbors went down the river to look for her. They had been looking for three days when the husband who had been away on a trip arrived. He was a mule driver. When he heard what had happened all he wanted to know was where the accident had occurred. Then the son-of-a-gun began to laugh as if he were being tickled. He said they were all just a pack of ninnies and knew nothing whatsoever about women. His old woman, he said, had always liked to go against the current, and so instead of looking for her down the river, they should have looked in the opposite direction. And they did; and they found her, good and dead, thirty leagues upstream."

The mestizos enjoyed the story, but the Indians, having no interpreter, were not listening. They all came to a place where the growth on the bank was so thick they could not examine it completely. There were some trees, leaning over the water like patient fishermen who have thrown in their lines. Doubtless the flood had swept over their lowest branches.

The leaders of the party ordered some of the Indians to swim out or to hold on to the rocks at the banks and rake through everything. Purple headed ducks arose with a whir from the most tangled places, and a few kingfishers were stirred up too. Downstream, among the boulders that had re-emerged now that the flood had gone down somewhat, a strange figure could be seen, apparently the body of a man. They all noticed the place at once, and went toward it in a hurry. But it was only the trunk of a tree, with two twisted limbs, rubbed white by the rocks.

Farther on, in a dark, very deep backwater, someone saw a blurred object, a suspicious shadow. It might be the body, held down by some heavy obstacle perhaps, for they all knew very well that by this time an unweighted corpse would be floating. One of the natives took off his shirt, his *huaraches*, and his hat, rolled up his trousers, and swam out into the hole.

He kept his direction by looking inquiringly at the men on the bank who were watching him from a high place. When they gave the signal agreed on he doubled like a beaver, ducked his head, threw his feet high in the air, and with a splash, disappeared for a long time.

When he came out, panting, and with his face flushed by the strain, he told them with signs that he had not found what they sought. Once out on the bank, he explained that what had deceived them was a branch of cottonwood which has leaves that are white underneath and glimmer like silver.

Downstream very far, already on the border of the next precinct, the searchers stopped, standing on what might be called the springboard of a waterfall. The river wound far away, tame in some stretches,

194

swift and foaming in others. When their eyes had become glutted with distance, they discovered—much closer, about a rifle-shot away—a buzzard swinging over the trees on the bank, at each swoop dropping until it almost touched the surface of the water, spying under some reeds that bent over the stream. After each peek, the buzzard would turn swiftly and float up again over the trees.

They all stood there watching closely. Once the buzzard, as it was taking flight again, lighted on a low branch, and stretched its neck out warily. Then it jumped as if, absurdly, it wanted to poise itself on the surface of the water, and came down carefully, wings raised. It plunged its beak in.

The searchers waited no longer. They clambered down over the rocks, went along the river bank, and when some were already pushing through the thicket, the buzzard flew up to one of the highest branches, gazing at them from there.

It was the corpse. A low branch, which had caught in his clothing, had stopped the dead man on his way to the sea. With no formality and accompanied by the noise of mestizos and the silence of the Indians, the body was taken to the bank,

195

where it was put on a smooth slab that looked like a tombstone.

They all recognized him at once, even though he was horribly swollen, and the minnows had chewed up his lips and eyelids. One of the mestizos, who knew about the feud between the two families, suggested that the tragedy might have been due to witchcraft, for how else could the best swimmer among them have been drowned?

That remark made the Indians draw off a little, apparently in fear that the corpse might still have some supernatural evil about it. And in the woods overlooking the waterfall, a strange figure appeared: bust of a man and legs of a child. He walked like the swinging of an unbalanced pendulum: it was the cripple, who had also been going up and down the river looking for his father.

XV. Revolution

SOMETHING very serious was happening among the *gente de razon.* Some of the Indians who had been working for the influential people in town brought news one day that a band of armed men had arrived suddenly, removed the authorities, and killed the military commander.

They, the Indians, had therefore left, especially as the new people did not seem to need them for anything. One old man said that when he was very young, he had been fortunate enough to witness some of the struggles among the whites, since they also war among themselves just as Indians do. He gave examples of family feuds, which are carried on in undying hatred, each side seeking to harm the other, even by witchcraft, until fathers and sons and their sons are all dead. The only difference between Indians and whites is this, said the old man: that the whites make war more efficiently, by means of the *amochitl*, the lead used in firearms.

Either from fear or because the officials and the hacienda owners did not call for their customary services, the Indians did no more work in the haciendas, much less go to their weekly shifts in town. Several months went by like this. Then the thunder of guns was heard for one whole night, and after that came an order to contribute fodder and tortillas because a large detachment of cavalry had entered the town.

So the Indians went down the road, one behind the other, like ants laying up provisions at the approach of the rainy season: some with a bundle of hay on their shoulders, others carrying baskets piled high with tortillas. The supplies were a tax levied on the rancheria and had been equally distributed among the inhabitants.

This went on for several weeks. The Indians were indifferent to what the struggling bands called themselves. They were guided by personal liking for some of the leaders, or merely by fear of the consequences if they disregarded orders.

One night they heard heavy firing again. It died down at dawn, but after daybreak the rattling went on without interruption for several hours. The defenders of the site were forced to retreat: so it was said by those who were by the road, and saw them pass hurriedly, in a sweat, stamped with the unmistakable air of people in flight. And thus passed, as the years went by, big detachments and little ones. . . .

A long time afterward one of the leaders climbed up to the village and broke the now customary calm of the heights, which the Indians had come to believe would last forever. What happened was that the head of a troop, not knowing the region, had lost himself during the hurried march. He demanded provisions, and also drafted a levy of twenty young men to serve him as "guides"; but he gave them rifles at once, and made them take the van. They never came back.

XVI. Plague

AFTER a season of excessive heat that destroyed the crops, a smallpox epidemic developed. Some thought it was the heat, while others started the story that the spirit of the *nahual* was trying to do away with them all. But both schools tried to fight the disease by the traditional methods: giving food to the hills, the winds and the waters; and taking *temaxcal* * baths, rubbing themselves with an herb which grows with its tiny leaves spread out on the ground and is therefore called *tianguis pepetla*, which means market-mat.

When the first deaths occurred, if a child was the victim, they had a dance with violin and *chirimia*; and if it was an adult, they held a wake in silence; but in either case they were not in the least dis-

---

* *Temaxcal*—native Indian steam bath, known in some form over most of pre-discovery America. Serves ceremonial and medicinal purposes and works on the same principle as the Turkish, Russian, and similar baths.

turbed by the idea of infection from their nearness to the black-pitted corpses.

Within a few days almost no one would go to wakes and funerals, even though the family might announce that there would be plenty of aguardiente. By that time, only the family itself sat with, buried, and mourned its own dead.

There was desolation in the rancheria. At night, barely one or two lights. From sunup, gray bundles huddled in the doorways: the sick Indians, rolled in their blankets, with only their eyes showing; still eyes on the dead landscape.

Then there were unburied corpses; and at that time, the cripple, as if showing that life held nothing for him and he did not fear death, gave water to the sick, and burial to the dead. In many cases, unable to carry the bodies, he dug graves for them inside the houses.

One day when he saw the house of his rival, the one who had taken his betrothed, closed, he risked inquiry. The door whined as it opened. The cripple put an ear in, listening. Then he said something in a low voice, as if pleading. When no one answered, he went in boldly.

He saw her on the *tlapextle*. The newborn child lay on the same bed. For a person with fever, what gift more welcome than cool water? The cripple filled the calabash from the water jar. He went over to give it to the sick woman, who seemed to be sleeping soundly. The child was asleep also. The cripple put the bowl on the floor. He stood over them like a weathered and twisted bronze statue: the head perfect, bowed by tormenting thoughts; the broad shoulders motionless; but what a painful contrast with his gnarled, shriveled legs!

He waited a long time and then put out the hand that was free of the crutch and touched the child's head lightly. He drew it back quickly: in that hot, fevered air, the child was cold. Then he looked more closely at the face of the woman—she who was to have been his wife—and then he knew the truth.

He shut himself in with her all afternoon, thinking and mourning, keeping the two bodies company. Having no one to help him, he made a grave next to the bed, rolled the bodies into it, and on top put the things dearest to the Indian woman: her marriage gourd, her bead necklaces, her *quexquemetl*, her girdle flecked with diamonds of yarn. Then he packed the earth down over them.

And silently, in the middle of the night, he closed the door.

∵

The natives could not help being surprised at one of the reasons given for the visit. They were accustomed from time immemorial to bear their afflictions alone. They had gone through the smallpox epidemic, with its losses, in the same mute manner as when the rancheria was lashed by the plague, year after year by dysentery, and almost chronically by *tzocoyote*,* which is what they call whooping cough because it is a baby's disease and *tzocoyote* is the nickname for the baby of the family.

The officials who notified the rancheria that the new deputy for the district was about to pay them a visit were careful to explain that this high functionary was taking so much trouble just to offer help to the sick, for news of the epidemic had reached the city. And, as the *tequihuis* had advised them that they were all obliged to remain at home all day Sun-

---

* *Tzocoyote,* also *xocoyote*—literally "little coyote."

day—some gave up a trip to the river and some to market—the representative of the people was received by a large crowd when he arrived.

He looked liked a guerrilla leader, with his important official air, his pistol at his belt, and riding a magnificent horse. When he was ready to dismount, no fewer than three hands reached for the reins: two were the municipal president's, and the third, his secretary's. Others in the party hurried to help the distinguished visitor off his horse.

The elders of the village approached and presented their respects. The young men remained in groups at some distance, waiting to do whatever might be ordered. The women peeked out through the chinks in the bamboo walls of their houses.

The deputy and his companions looked at the rancheria with the same sort of attention that all curious travelers give to places they have never seen before. The fatigue of the horses, covered with dust and sweat, betrayed the difficult condition of the road, requiring the same number of hours it would have taken to cover five times the distance. The amazed faces said only one thing: what backwardness!

204

To escape the heat, the visitors sat down under a leafy tree. They were all fanning themselves with their hats; and they asked for water. As many old men as there were thirsty mouths brought bright-colored gourds filled to the brim. When he felt more comfortable, the deputy told them how pleased he was that the smallpox epidemic was over; at least, as far as he could see, for he had not noticed a single face with fresh scabs on it. What he saw was the collective face of the rancheria, all covered with perfectly scarred pocks. The number of pock-marked Indians revealed better than anything the appalling extent of the disease.

Someone in the deputy's party had an idea when he saw the young natives waiting idly; as the saying goes, "because he sees the horse saddled, he has to travel." He suggested that they go get hay for the horses, which could easily be fed during the visit. No one objected; they even added that the Indians could also unsaddle and water the horses.

Moreover, the elders were told that the deputy and his companions had decided to stay for dinner. They therefore ordered the *tequihuis* to arrange everything. Three or four of the principal houses contributed the chickens and the turkeys; other villagers provided enough maize for the tortillas; still others brought plenty of beans; someone brought salt; and the women set to work.

And, while they were preparing the meal, the meeting, which was the main purpose of the visit, was organized. It was decided to hold it in the gallery that was used for the *tianguis* and holiday dances. The natives, a compact and numerous crowd in which the white of cotton and hats predominated, surrounded the visitors. A *mexcatl*, as they call those who speak their language well, listened to the deputy's instructions, and then began explaining to the Indians the reason for the gathering.

He told them that the deputy, notwithstanding the hard road and his many affairs in the city, had decided to visit the rancheria, because he wanted to bring them the good news of the situation: which was that, now the liberating movement had triumphed, he wanted to teach them how to be free; that the revolution, which had been made at the cost of so many lives, had been made for them, for the Indians; and also, hearing of the smallpox epidemic, he had wanted to see things for himself, even at the risk of catching the disease.

The interpreter went on to say that the visit of the deputy established a precedent in the history of the district, for when had they ever looked upon the face of one of those lordly officials appointed during the now happily departed dictatorship? Those men had not known even the location of the districts they represented, let alone the people in them.

The Indians listened, making no sign of contradiction or approval; with their racial indifference, face of stone and eyes of opaque glass. The interpreter, swallowing a gourdful of water, talked to the deputy again. Then he renewed his harangue, saying that the impressions made on the deputy had begun to bear fruit, for he was already planning to bring progress to the rancheria, to build a road, to put up a school: the first in order to bring about the commercial development of the region, and the second, so that from now on the Indians would be able to speak the tongue of the whites.

Two words in his ear made him quickly include a reservation: that the federal government, busy as it was attending to other and more important places, could not take charge of these works; the district government, on account of its poverty, also was not the proper agency, since its income was hardly enough to pay for the salaries and services of the municipal president, secretary, magistrate, judge of the lower courts, clerks, teachers, postal employees, police, lighting, et cetera. . . .

The natives may have been thinking that from these services, toward which they paid imposts and head-tax, they got no benefit. But no one said a word. So the spokesman of the deputy went on to make a request: that the men of the rancheria, as well as all the other Indians, contribute two days of work a week in order to open the highway. And, since it was impossible to put up a school and support a teacher in each rancheria, one school would be built some place equally near the biggest villages, so that all the children could attend, with just the slight inconvenience of walking a few kilometers daily.

The natives, uncommunicative or pessimistic, said nothing. The elders had to be asked for their opinion. They ventured the statement that all who were already giving gratuitous services in weekly shifts in the town, or those who, though paid, were already engaged in forced labor on the haciendas, might not be able to discharge all these new duties too.

The moment he heard that there existed such outrages on their liberty, the deputy burst into a speech, addressing the Indians without the interpreter; but when he realized that they did not understand him, he again gave instructions to the *mexcatl*. The latter explained that it was now decreed that every man who was giving domestic service in the house of a town functionary was hereby released, so that he could go and work on the highway. As to being drafted to work by the day on the haciendas, they must not submit to it, for "no one is obligated to give personal services without just recompense and his full consent." For emphasis, the deputy made the interpreter quote the corresponding article in the Constitution, which the *mexcatl* translated in his own way.

Dinner was served where the meeting had been held. Stools to sit on and boards for tables were brought from all the houses. The deputy made some of the elders sit next to him. The rest of the natives acted as waiters. Of the women, only a few old ones appeared, bringing food.

What the deputy praised most were the delicious tortillas made of black maize.

XVII. The Lost Tradition

WHEN the preliminary work on the highway began, a serious difficulty arose in
the rancheria, as in others of the region.
The priest was traveling from village to village in
the mountains, telling the people to build churches,
because the smallpox epidemic had been sent to punish them for their impiety.

He did not mention the highway; he was not
interested. What he did say was that the church
should be begun at once, because otherwise who
knows what further misfortunes might rain down on
the villages.

The elders met for a discussion of the problem:
on the one hand there was the order to start opening the road; and on the other, the divine threat,
the danger that the word of the priest might become
a reality. It was impossible to obey the two man-
dates at the same time. Some of the old men, who
proposed that the forces be divided, and an equal

number of workers be assigned to each job, seemed to dominate the council. But to avoid responsibility, the elders solved the problem in another way: two days for the authorities, and two days for . . . the other authorities. Four days of the week without rest and without wages.

∴

It was a surprise to the Indians when they found that the highway, following the survey already made, would not go to their rancheria, but would cut through the valley to who knows where.

The *cues, cubes* or *tzacuales* — archeological mounds—became inexhaustible sources of building stone, as they had been for centuries. There was over a kilometer of highway already down, and the workers had scarcely used up one mound. The *cues* date from time so remote that when the highway was started, and the first mound attacked, the Indians had to chop away great trees and a thick layer of vegetation growing on the crude archeological structure.

The stone humps, rough pyramids as big as a house, seemed to trace a route across the valley.

Diego Rivera

The chain was cut when it reached the mountains, but began again beyond. It might have marked a road, an ancient road that dated from centuries and centuries ago.

One was tempted to ask the stones what hands had shaped them and heaped them like chronological milestones. And, getting no answer, one wanted to ask the other survivals from the past, those who now came and went with the sacred burdens on their backs.

And the oldest would reply:

"It was the *huchues.*"

Meaning the old ones, the forebears. And as to what the mounds were for, he would answer that perhaps the grandfathers knew. . . .

The legends say that, when the tribal priests received a new order to march on, they put aside the gods, the household goods and implements, and everything they could not carry, building over them the rough pyramid to serve as some sort of a protection or as a sign. Others say that when the old men were told that the world was coming to an end by a flood, they built the *cues*, putting their possessions and those of each family, inside, sure that in

215

the next life they would find them: the hunter his arrows; the women their spinning whorls. . . .

But who knows? The tradition has been lost. . . .

The picks hit a great slab, making a strange sound. The foreman came closer and the workers withdrew. When the rock was lifted, there appeared a black and porous idol, a shattered comal, several spinning whorls, and a metate.

One of the peons advised them not to come too close right away, for the spirits of the ancestors live in the *cues*, and they might get angry: one must wait till they awaken and leave. The overseer replied that this was just a pretext not to work, and in support of what he said, and of his own unbelief, he trampled on the find, crushing the fragments of the terra-cotta-colored comal under his heels.

Then with some difficulty he picked up the idol and stood it upright against a rock. The idol was about a yard high, with a big head, flat nose and thick legs. It was one of those that in rich archeological regions turn up in stone fences like an ordinary rock.

The workers went back to their task. They seemed angry or afraid, and while they hauled

216

stones back and forth, one who was crushing the big slabs said that he knew of many cases, some happy and some sad, having to do with *cues:* one *coyotl,* that is, a white, was left paralyzed, motionless as a rock, all because he had awakened some of the gods of the grandfathers before their time. But another, when he smashed an idol, found it full of gold dust inside. . . .

The overseer seemed much more interested in the latter. He looked at the idol more closely. Then he took a pick and struck the figure on the head. As the stone triumphantly resisted, he struck it again, at the middle of the body. Finally, he managed to break off an arm. He hit the image furiously, without stopping, until it broke in two at the waist.

Instead of gold there was nothing but black and porous rock, volcanic most likely, as new as in its geological childhood. Disappointed, the overseer sent the pieces of the idol rolling down the short slope.

$$\cdot\;\cdot$$

The workers' tools gave off silvery reflections at a distance. Hundreds of Indians from the neighbor-

ing rancherias were working actively on the first
cut of the highway. Some turned up the earth with
crowbars in a strip pegged out by the helpers of the
amateur engineers. Others, flourishing spades,
pitched the fresh earth into the fields; beyond, still
others packed the roadway down with huge
pounders. Much farther away, so far they could
scarcely be seen, there were more workers laying and
fitting the stones; and, winding through all of them,
the chain bringing rock from the *cues:* brown ants
glistening with sweat.

The town officials came to inspect the work in
the afternoons. The delegation would ride in on
horseback among the Indians, and the highest official would deign to speak to them in a friendly manner, encouraging them. He would enumerate to his
companions the great advantages that the new route
would bring to the region. And all this done through
his own personal efforts, for the central government
gave no help at all. Finally, as if to protect himself from some danger, he would add:

"Naturally. The federal government has many
other things to attend to. This region is one of the
most isolated. It is the duty of all who are revolu-

218

tionists at heart to do something on their own initiative."

At times, in order to soothe the Indians, he would say to the elders that they must not imagine that they would have to finish the road by themselves. He would not dream of sacrificing his constituents like that. He had already made arrangements with the authorities of adjoining districts for their inhabitants to take charge of continuing the work.

On Saturday afternoons, to give lavish relief to the tired Indians, the municipal president would send two barrels of aguardiente, from which was distributed as much as two glasses to each workman. Meanwhile, he would talk with great satisfaction of how easy it was to make works of progress. The proof was right here, on this very highway, with which his friend, the deputy, the intellectual author of the work, would be highly pleased.

"What used to be covered in two days on horseback soon will be made comfortably in two hours by automobile. *Si, señor!* In two hours!"

∴

The Indians wondered to themselves how it was that the priest had ordered the building of the church, when they were so busy with the road. They could have made it comfortably at any other time, taking two days a week, for a good many months.

Seen from the mountains during the hottest hours of the day, the highway was beginning to look like a long strip of cotton cloth spread out to dry in the valley. On the church, the foundation was ready. The stone had to be brought in from a distance, and without the facilities of the *cues*. No doubt their forefathers struggled with these same difficulties when they made their mounds, for there was not much rock in the valley. And in the hills it took streams of sweat to quarry and shape it.

But the most curious part of it all was that the reverend father, having left the cords stretched to mark the plan of the building, went off without paying any more attention to it; as if all he had wanted was to take them away from the work ordered by the authorities. It was only fear that made them finish the highway and continue with the church. The fields were full of weeds, choking the maize. Some of the elders had already called attention to the fact that day after day long strands of hawks crossed the sky, migrating to other lands, a sure sign of coming hunger.

220

XVIII. The Pilgrims

Soon after they had finished their share of the highway the Indians were ordered to bring materials for building the school to a settlement in the approximate center of the region.

But they had barely begun on the school when still another order interrupted the work and delayed the completion of the building: the priest had gone through all the rancherias of the parish, saying that he could no longer tolerate that time should pass and that a debt should remain unpaid; a sacred debt that he had contracted in the name of his faithful.

He explained that at the height of the recent epidemic, he had made a vow that all the survivors would join in a grateful pilgrimage to a certain miraculous saint whose protection he had invoked, asking that they be healed. They had not known about the petition, he added; but, all the same and without question, that was the reason the smallpox had not wiped them out completely. He was telling them now, because he was anxious that the debt should be paid. Otherwise it might well happen that, when the epidemic returned, the saint would not listen.

There was some uncertainty among the natives: on the one hand, the order of the authorities to build a school; on the other, the threat, the word of the *totatzi,** pointing out the possible consequences of religious bankruptcy.

The old men had to ponder over this, so they called a meeting. After long deliberation experience spoke. The aged, the children and the women, except those who were needed to feed the workers, would all go on the pilgrimage, while the able-bodied men would remain to lend a hand with the building, the first step of the educational program of the deputy.

As the date of the yearly festival, dedicated to the miraculous image, was very near, preparations for the pilgrimage were begun at once. There was so much activity in the rancheria that from the first night no one slept any more. It must have been in this way the tribes prepared to migrate when, hav-

---

* *Totatzi*—"representative of God" in Aztec.

ing lived in one place for a long time, the summons came to move on; following the winged chant, that in the days of exodus was like a goad and a hope in one.

The women devoted themselves to packing the bundles necessary for eight days of absence: three to go, three to come back, and two in the town. One week of travel to give thanks to the saint for the health granted them. Those who were going looked forward to it gaily: strange roads, other people, and new horizons.

The men prepared the *huaraches* for themselves, their wives and their children; a task that is nearly always superfluous, for once on the road, the Indian hangs his sandals from the provision sack, and feels much more comfortable barefoot. The same kind of thing happens with a new hat which, when it rains, is sheltered under the blanket to keep it from getting wet.

The elders collected money among all the villagers for the expenses of the trip, as well as to buy the wax candles and the ex-votos with which they would pay homage to the miraculous image.

Anxious to please the saint, they took the members of the ritual dance group and the musicians from among the men who could well have remained at work. They decided that this would be one more tribute to the saint.

To build up general enthusiasm, or else because some rehearsal was necessary, the musicians and dancers began to organize themselves. Together the performers went from door to door. The rancheria looked as if it were celebrating a holiday, and it was indeed: this was a kind of first fruits for the saint, a greeting at a distance, more effective perhaps than the prayer of the priest.

And at last, one dawn, squads of pilgrims left the rancheria. Out on the road they fell into single file, traveling with that typically Indian, resigned trot and seeming not to know how to raise their eyes from the dust. It was a moving cordon wearily swinging, in the sun, in the rain. It would take three days for them to get to the town where the shrine was and offer their gifts of atonement to the image, pleading like a tardy debtor who excuses himself to his patron.

It was a line of children's feet, still tender for the calcined earth and the rocky hills; women's feet, harder from the household routine; and the bear's feet of the men, scarred and cracked by their habitual trotting. A line of heads bowed from the habit of carrying burdens; hair white and black, with no shades between, never a brown or a blonde; black-maned heads. A whole tribe, that could have founded a town. . . .

At noon they stopped at a waterhole. They gathered wood from the side of the road, and made fires to warm their food. They ate sitting on the ground; then drank at the arroyo, and went on their way.

That night they asked permission at a ranch to sleep in the outside corridors of the main house. There they spread out their blankets and fell asleep in the open air, together, one big family. Then very early, with the first light of day, they measured up how far they had come, and how far they had to go. And thus, chattering like a flock of parrots in flight, they took up their march toward the town that owes its fame to the reputation of the saint shrined in its church.

When they arrived at this town, which in their eyes was like some kind of enchanted place, the fiestas had already begun. They had been greeted by the pealing of bells when they could barely be seen coming around the bends in the sierra road. All together, like fowls being driven through city streets to market, they went straight to the church.

Who knows what echoes were roused in the souls of the Indians by the ringing bells, the organ music and the chanting? Surely they were dazzled by the altars, transformed into great centers of light. Jammed in the door of the church, the tribe was like the jungle itself, breathless with amazement. Their attitude, though they were not on their knees, was the symbol of humility itself.

The priest who had ordered them to make this thanksgiving pilgrimage to the fiesta of the saint saw them standing and peremptorily, pushing on their shoulders, made them kneel.

When the mass was over and the nave was being emptied of worshipers, the same priest took the tribe to the altar of the miraculous saint. They gave thanks on their knees for the health granted them, but their lips did not move: they implored with their eyes. The priest then exacted whatever they had, for charity and candles.

226

The dancers, lined up at one side of the temple, entered in perfect formation, and for some hours gave homage to the deities in the only language they knew: music and dancing; but not as on the secular holiday of the rancheria; instead, full of intuitive devotion.

For the money and the offerings, the Indians got relics which they hung around their necks, burned by a sun that first rose on their race before the exodus, was at the zenith when the white men arrived in the new world, and still blazes. That night the tribe slept huddled like a flock in the atrium.

∴

It took a long time to build the school, but it was relatively easy, because of the way the work was distributed. The men who lived near the jungle brought the beams and the bamboo; those from the cooler slopes, where the cereals grow, brought hay in big sheaves for the thatch; some brought lumber for doors and benches; others, stone for the foundation and the corridor. The school was made like a big hut, with white walls, and eaves like trimmed beards.

227

The deputy, when he heard that the school was finished, ordered the municipal president to put the name of some distinguished benefactor or national hero over the door. And the municipal president then arranged that the name over the door should be that of the deputy himself, saying it was only fair, since the school was his work.

XIX. The Leader

THE first teacher who arrived to take charge of the school was a young man who came from a town in the region, and who, finding it impossible to get to the city in order to continue his studies and train for a profession, had resigned himself to the modest career of rural school teacher.

The attendance was large at first, since the town officials had ordered all heads of families to send their children, even if they had to walk several kilometers a day. All the peasant children of the region converged on the place very early in the morning, coming from various directions and over many trails: the poor afoot, the children of the rich on burros.

But the schoolmaster soon realized that in order to develop an effective program he would have to form two groups: one, the children of the mestizos and whites, who spoke Spanish; and the other, the

Indians who spoke only their own language. He explained how it was to the authorities, detailing to the point of weariness that the Indians badly needed a teacher who spoke their own language. But the authorities objected on the grounds of expense, the poverty of the local budget, and said that the children of the natives would learn Spanish soon enough.

So then the teacher concentrated his energy on accumulating a vocabulary of Indian words. He would ask his pupils the names of things, and write them down in a notebook. He was trying to provide himself with the essential instrument—the language—but when he wanted to use it, the words he had written down were not of much use to him. He tried another method, or rather the same one reversed: to teach his pupils Spanish, and thus be able to communicate his other knowledge.

Every time he talked to the authorities and the townspeople, he called their attention to the urgent need of giving special training to the rural teachers and of providing them with complete vocabularies. Enthused with what he called his "educational plan for liquidating the illiteracy of the Indian," he would suggest the necessity of compiling as many dictionaries as there are native languages and dialects in the country: Nahuatl, Otomi, Totonac, Tepehua, Chamula, Tarascan, etc. A hundred vocabularies. In a word, do what the missionaries had done: first learn the native language, in order then to teach the language of the Conquest.

But the young schoolmaster was not able to put together even an average vocabulary of the language which part of his pupils spoke. Therefore he devoted his entire attention to the children of the mestizos, from whom he was not separated by any such barriers. Neglected, the children of the Indians wasted their time.

In this somewhat barren ground, the teacher began to be bored. He missed the life of the town, which he had now only on Sundays. It is true that the natives gave him a kind of bonus, cultivating a piece of earth for him, as ordered by the authorities; but he had other ambitions. When his work was over, he would wander through the fields like a ghost. He talked to himself. And he even got to the point of writing verses to a non-existent sweetheart; which did not prevent him one afternoon from chasing, like a he-goat, after a young Indian girl, who slipped easily from his hands.

A few months after the school was founded, the attendance had diminished about seventy per cent. The youngest children could not stand the long daily hikes, and the bigger ones were kept at home by their parents to work. Only the children of mestizo farmer families, who were better off and had more confidence in the school, kept on coming.

Finally, complaining of the heat, and of what he called the crudeness of the natives, the teacher resigned to take a position as clerk in the town, where, as he said, at least he would be dealing with *gente de razon*.

The best explanation of the schoolmaster's flight was given by an Indian whose son had been drafted as a soldier many years ago. He said he had had no word of the boy for two years and had finally decided he was lost forever; and he was, at least to him and to the rancheria.

He had finally got news of the boy when he went to market in town one Sunday. He was going to buy something to offer up on the approaching Days of the Dead, when the houses are festooned with marigold and altars are spread with the favorite dishes of the loved dead. One of the prominent men of the town, who visited the city now and then on business, told him the boy was alive, and that he was a soldier. He had got this information from an officer in the same company.

With great hope of accumulating the necessary money to pay a substitute, the old man began to work, economizing in every possible way that he could, and selling what little he owned. A year later he asked the merchant to do him the favor of soliciting his son's discharge the next time he went to the city. And he gave him the money to make the necessary payment. Then joyfully he looked forward to his son's return.

The merchant carried out the commission faithfully. Once in the city, he looked for his friend the officer, and together they went to the barracks and talked with the boy. They did not talk in the native language any more, but in Spanish. The merchant gave the soldier the good news. He told him about the money he had brought, and that they were going to apply for his discharge. But the soldier

233

heard it all without the slightest sign of pleasure. Finally, he said:

"Tell my father that I am grateful for his pains and trouble to bring about my return and that I realize the effort he must have made to get this money together. But I shall not use it, and I am returning it so that he may enjoy it. Tell him that I am contented as a soldier. I have learned to read and write, I wear shoes and other clothing, I hope to be promoted soon, and I would not be happy back there. . . ."

And the old man would add:

"That is what has happened to this professor: he was not happy here, because he misses other people and other customs."

It was about this time that a school inspector had a brilliant idea. For positions in the rural schools attended by Indians, preference should be given to young men of the same race who, besides having had adequate training, knew both languages.

They carried the idea out and for that region chose a young Indian who was at that time secretary in a court of first instance. No one like him, they thought, for the job of incorporating the peo-

234

ple of his own race into the civilized world. The inspector, discussing the fortunate discovery, said that the young man would be the best possible link between copper-colored and white.

He was very well known locally. His parents had been servants in a near-by hacienda. He had been left an orphan, and the master—rightfully so —took charge of him; or rather, took him into his personal service. When the landowner had to flee from the revolution, he took the boy as well as other servants along with him. In town he was generous enough to send him to school. The boy, whose tongue still tripped over the new language, would say, when the teacher called the roll, *"Prisente,"* instead of *"Presente."*

The master, who was a very devout man, thought he would send the boy to a religious seminary as soon as he was old enough and knew enough to take this training. The boy, on the other hand, would say that he wanted to be a lawyer. But another revolutionary wave flooded the valley and rose up to the hills until it reached the town; so the landlord had to flee for the second time. The adopted son was left behind to visit the hacienda occa-

235

sionally and to look after his foster-father's city property.

This was the man who was to be the new teacher for the rural school. Offered a higher salary than he was receiving in the court, he accepted. His own people were very happy to see him, and he was enthusiastic over the prospect of what he might accomplish for them.

When he saw that no native children attended, he visited the rancherias, and there it was thoroughly explained to him: to cultivate the earth was much more urgent than to cultivate their children. Besides, children eat too—said one Indian burdened with a large family—and, therefore, they also have to work. They made clear to him the time wasted going back and forth to school. One of the old men came to the conclusion that when there is not enough to eat, schools are a luxury. More than anything else, the new teacher was deeply struck by the inequalities that oppressed the Indians. For example, every Indian from the moment he reached the age when he was barely able to perform the simplest chores was enrolled as a taxpayer by the precinct judges in charge of collecting the head-tax; while the teacher knew the liberal policy practiced toward the people of the town.

On his way back to the school, afoot, over the trails of the sierra, where the legendary splendor of the Indian past lives on only in the trees and the birds, he thought much about his race. Leaning against a huge slab of granite, he ran his fingers over his beardless jaw, his high cheekbones, his straight hair; and he looked at his copper-colored hands. . . . To think that he hadn't concerned himself with his people before! He had heard many times in the town that the peasants had been given land to help them economically, but now that he came in contact with them again, he realized that land isn't everything. Many tribes, like his, had held their own land for centuries, yet they continued in poverty and ignorance.

Motionless, he leaned against the same rock for a long time, in the same position, and let his eyes travel over the mountains and the valley. He did not have to ask about the economic condition of his people. The picture was spread out before him.

The dense dark green of the forest was dominant in the vast landscape: uncultivated, idle lands.

Much lower down, huge squares, rhomboids, triangles—the big plantations: green pastures where the favorite places of the cattle showed yellowish; the less frequented brakes, a dull green. Stretches of deep, even emerald: the cane nearly ready to be cut. At one side, dun fields, almost brown: the landlord's maize, planted at the proper time, now showing the first signs of ripeness. In other parts, like tranquil lakes, the unreal blue-green of tobacco.

And on the hills, the cultivated patches of the Indians, like penny postage stamps on great colored envelopes. Their size revealed how little time the owners could give them during the best season for clearing and sowing. It was a personal effort, the work of one man. One could see by their new-straw tinge that they did not get the rains in time and that the drought had ripened them prematurely.

He calculated the number of inhabitants in the rancheria; then he counted the small fields: one patch for every five persons.

He stayed there for a long time and thought a great deal more: whether it was the many demands of the whites which did not permit his people to better themselves; or if, after all, as he had heard

238

so many times, their misery was due to their own shiftlessness.

∵

When he looked at his pupils, the schoolmaster realized that he was not going to teach Indians like himself, but children of the creoles, the land workers who lived in the lowlands, but were a step higher in the social scheme than the Indians. The difference is measured by the levels of the rancherias; they correspond to the traditional fear between the creoles and the Indians, which, fed by persecution and exploitation, is like the thermometer of mistrust. The Indians, who in their obscure wanderings went along the banks of the rivers and founded cities in the valleys, had retreated into the sierras from the domination of the whites; and now came down only when persuaded by confidence.

When he made up his program the teacher thought mainly in terms of a social scheme. He had learned from his people that they were paying the head-tax, legally abolished; it was necessary then to expose this, even at the cost of making the town officials his enemies. They had also told him

239

that the land they had received had not improved their economic situation, partly because they were not equipped to cultivate it properly, but also for lack of time, due to the demands of the authorities. So one must ask for subsidies to carry out the work, financial backing so that the Indian farmer should not fall into the hands of those who buy his produce in the field. Tools must be bought and teachers engaged, to wipe out the old agricultural methods. They had told him that they often had to give their products away because there was no transportation to take them to market: therefore, a road was necessary, but not like the one they had put through the valley to connect who knows what different points, along which the Indian travels afoot, enveloped in dust; rather, a road that would be an outlet for the tribes, now isolated as always by their ancient racial fears. . . .

His ideas and plans, put before a council of the elders, greatly alarmed them; they were of the opinion that such demands would bring new conflicts upon them. They were already weary of persecution, and met all promise of betterment skeptically.

In his own way, the schoolmaster explained the

spirit of the new laws. And, to arouse confidence in his people, he told them that the highest officials of the government were about to redeem all the peasants, especially the Indians, with schools and economic changes, such as the distribution of land. The rudiments of law that he had acquired in his job in the court helped him to present this argument.

The white heads of the elders remained sunk on their naked and bony chests for a long time, as they tried to reach a decision. The wrinkled, beardless faces in doubt betrayed nothing. They were like carved wood. But the teacher shook them with the least important of his promises, which was however the most immediate and effective: to get the head-tax abolished!

Finally the oldest one spoke. He said that the teacher's youth did not qualify him to give advice; but that since he had lived among the whites, wore shoes and city pants, and furthermore, knew how to read and write, there might be something to what he said. And they all put themselves in his hands. Thus ended a very ancient tradition.

The young man wrote a long memorial to the governor of the state, in which he courageously complained that the local authorities were still collecting the head-tax from the Indians. He also took advantage of the opportunity to complain that his people were still obliged to give personal services, without pay, as domestics in the houses of the wealthy; but above all, in shifts on road repair work, on building jobs in town, and on the sugar-cane haciendas.

He did not have to wait long for an answer. It was in the form of a copy of the communication sent by the governor to the municipal president of the district, informing him of the complaint, and ordering him, in the name of revolutionary ideals, to cease collecting the head-tax.

When the schoolmaster translated the contents of the document to his people, even the oldest showed signs of respect for him who, by the mere writing of a paper, had succeeded in taking an ancient burden from their shoulders. Encouraged by his success, the schoolmaster revealed his intentions further: to go with a large delegation to the city and there ask, through the deputy, for better lands than those of the rancheria and for agricultural implements; but especially for arms with which to defend themselves, since he was sure that the people of the town would become their enemies.

Thus, concrete achievement brought the Indians together, and a leader came forward among them.

XX. Politics

EVERYTHING that the leader had promised his people he got for them by tenacity and boldness. He relied most on the state deputy from his district who, as soon as he realized that the young Indian had the makings of an agitator, made a close friend of him. The deputy went with the leader and his delegation to the government palace, to the agrarian committee, and to every public man whose influence might be of advantage.

The leader had no sooner returned from his last trip to the city than instructions arrived to take his men to two rancherías near by, and there to organize the inhabitants for defense. A White Guard * had just been formed to reoccupy the land that until a short time ago had belonged to the hacendado and had now been broken up according to the agrarian policy of the new government.

---

* White Guard—*guardia blanca,* name given to private troops and police employed by owners of property.

The defenders started eagerly, hoping for a chance to try out their newly acquired arms. If only they could have had them when the strangers outraged the girl and tormented the guide who took them to the hills in search of the mine and medicinal plants! All three adventurers would have been left in the canyon, not just one.

Now they were men: that is what a gun and authority will do. They went along jauntily, and when they met whites on the highway they looked them in the eye. Even the vehicles, that used to endanger their lives and cover them with dust, were now careful to slow down; the weapons were a warning. The troop, which included all the able-bodied men of the rancheria, was impressive. The Indians gave yells of pure savage joy. A few drinks at a roadside stand excited them more and more.

The other rancheria received them with enthusiasm. That same afternoon there was a meeting. Their young leader announced that he bore written orders from higher up; he expressed his friendship and loyalty for the deputy; and then asked for a detailed account of the quarrel.

It seemed that the inhabitants of this rancheria,

who had been accustomed to working on certain haciendas, had occupied the land as he had told them
to do. Then they had wanted other ground which
they thought was better; and then the landowner
had threatened them with his White Guard. They
were ready to defend themselves, they added, but
they had no guns. . . .

The old men and the leader talked things over.
After that he said that at dawn he would give them
the land himself. There was a big feast and a dance
in his honor that night. They entertained him as
the deputy himself had been entertained when he
visited the rancheria.

At dawn the Indians began to come down from
the hills, toward the valley. They came down as
they had in other times, on their way to the river,
to fish, or to search for wild fruits. But then they
had carried net and spear; now it was rifle and machete. When they came to the hacienda, they cut
the fence wires, made openings as boundary mark-
ers, and took possession. Just then a group of armed
men appeared. It was the White Guard.

The shooting lasted twenty minutes. The natives
and their attackers, shielded by tree trunks, had only

two casualties. Both bands retreated cautiously, carrying their dead on improvised stretchers. The struggle had now actually begun. At a great mass meeting that night, the Indians decided to solicit more arms, and to ask the higher-ups—at least the deputy—for more positive instructions.

Then the economic problem came up; trips to the city cost money. The leader levied a quota on each head of a family. Some objected that the struggle was unnecessary, that they had enough with the lands already obtained. But the leader was upheld; he said that it was not just a matter of lands any more, but of principle. And he left, taking a large delegation along.

With the committee went Indians bearing presents for the powerful political supporters of the leader: one carried a big-crested turkey for three days to be given to his honor the deputy; another had fat hens for his honor the governor; the rest brought choice maize and new beans for other influential gentlemen.

In the old days, these same presents used to go to the local boss and the lawyer.

The landlord also, they heard later, went to the

247

city to defend his rights. There being two different versions of what had happened, the authorities said that the case would be carefully investigated. The officials seemed to be sick and tired of conflicts like this. The deputy promised the committee to keep after the matter; and, in return, the leader would continue controlling the rancherias: the elections were approaching, and the deputy wanted a seat in the national congress.

Within two weeks orders came to organize all the people. The deputy planned to hold a great demonstration at the district seat to show his vast popularity, his identification with the humble, and to launch his electoral campaign. In the same letter the deputy said to the Indian leader that, considering his many qualities, he had taken the liberty of putting him on the ticket as his alternate.

With such prospects, the leader redoubled his activities. He told his people that this mere possibility was already a promise of betterment for all: to have a political representative of their own race. So now none of them would dream of refusing any commission, no matter how dangerous.

Indians converged on the town from all the

sierras on the day of the demonstration. The roads were white with palm hats. They crossed the valley. They filled the streets. The crowd went through the middle of the town toward the other side, where the deputy, candidate for a seat in the federal assembly, was welcomed with fireworks and a blaring band.

The rival candidate, who had also organized a demonstration but could count only on the townspeople and some from the haciendas, had to retreat to the city hall. The first orator to address the throng was the Indian leader, who stood with the deputy at his right. He made a long speech in the tongue of his people: land, food, arms, agricultural implements, credit, et cetera.

A considerable number of the demonstrators were drunk by the afternoon, and the town looked as if it had been occupied by an army. The houses of the people supposed to be the leading citizens stayed closed. The multitude saw the deputy off, and left in an uproar.

Wherever the trails forked groups split off toward their own villages. Back in the rancheria, the leader frankly told his men, before they scattered, that his

249

friend, the deputy, needed money to carry on his campaign; and that every head of a family would have to contribute his share.

∴

The news alarmed them: the leader was notified that the landowner's White Guard, in combination with the authorities of the town, intended to take the rancheria by surprise, burn the houses, and kill the new politician, who was now regarded as a real menace, in view of the demonstration of strength on the day of the parade through the streets.

The first step was to call a meeting. The leader said that the advantages they had gained had angered the old bosses; and that he was in the most dangerous position, as they intended to kill him; but he was always ready to sacrifice himself for his people—a phrase he had picked up faithfully from the deputy—and that now was the time when they all, with no exception whatsoever, must help to the utmost. He ended saying how much he regretted having to ask for more money to buy ammunition in order to be ready for a real battle.

The rancheria was transformed into an armed

Diego Rivera. 36

camp.   Rock barricades, like trenches, were raised at the entrances.   Advance outposts, also protected by stone walls, were put at strategic points on the roads, and those who had firearms were stationed there. The cripple, being insignificant, was sent down to watch from the bushes at the edge of the highway, and signal if the enemy approached.   A lookout, who was on a ledge like a balcony at the highest part of the sierra, would pick up the signal.

Couriers went out daily in different directions: messages for concentration, orders, counter-orders, letters to the deputy, protests to the authorities. . . . Actually, there were two fronts: the war on the White Guard, and the electoral campaign.

The *huehues*, spokesmen for caution, but also for weakness, advised flight as always: to take, as in other times of panic, the most tangled trails; seek safety in the ancient shelter of a cave or a hut deep in the forest.   But the leader had his way.

In the end, word came that the White Guard had been notified from very high up, that in case of any more bloodshed, they would be held responsible, since they were attempting to undermine the strength of one of the candidates in the primaries.

253

Besides which, it was already known that they had been the aggressors in the last encounter.

The essential idea of giving land to the majority, in order to help them economically, was being pushed to the background by politics. Long cordons of workers, native and mestizo, traveled all the roads, taken back and forth by leaders to show their strength to the politicians still higher up.

A whole pyramiding of interests: comings and goings of peasants to the meetings prior to the general elections; pilgrimages in support of the candidate for governor; fields abandoned because it was necessary to go to the seat of the district and give the candidate for deputy a rousing welcome; concentrations to defend the cause of the municipal president; groups supporting an alderman; committees to ask for another.agrarian delegate; a trip to keep the precinct judge from being removed. . . . And, back of the peasants, the leaders driving the flock.

In the conflict of so many interests, a new style of attack arose: the ambush. The rancheria would hear every day of bloody and unpunished assaults: a volley from the forest, to obliterate an official, a landowner, or an Indian.

254

On election day, when long lines of Indians went through the fields on their way to town, the old men, as they passed the best lands, lamented not having had time to clear them, let alone to sow. The words *cintli* and *etl*, the maize and the bean, were pronounced with a certain fear: the traditional fear of a people that has suffered hunger.

XXI. Distrust

THE CRIPPLE still spies from his hiding-place in the brambles. Distrust itself, as he looks out on the highway—civilization. High on the mountain, the sentinel waits for the signal. Like the rest of their people, all they know is that the *gente de razon* want to attack them. That hatreds snarl in packs in the valley and the sierra. And that, in the city, the leader is well taken care of.